Praise for
SAUL WILLIAMS

"Saul Williams is the prototype synthesis between poetry and hip-hop, stage and page, rap and prose, funk and mythology, slam and verse. . . . He avoids classifications, and empowers the human voice."

—Mark Eleveld, author of *The Spoken Word Revolution: Slam, Hip Hop and the Poetry of the Next Generation*

"[Saul's] a profound poet who inspires us. He challenges us to be individuals."

—Russell Simmons

"One of the finest minds in the country has put pen to paper, voice to verse, and dug into the deep, rich planet better known as the souls of black folks."

—Nelson George

"Saul is every kind of great artist combined into one. He is the best of every genre in one."

—Nas

"One of the most recognizable poets in America, and [he] has established a worldwide fan base with his magnetic spoken-word performance. . . . With a lexicon matched by few, Williams illuminates hip-hop's golden era while setting sights on the future."

—Tyson Wheatley, CNN

Also by
SAUL WILLIAMS

Chorus (editor)

The Dead Emcee Scrolls

, said the shotgun to the head.

She

US (a.)

SAUL WILLIAMS

THIS BOOK IS A GIFT FROM THE FRIENDS OF THE ORINDA LIBRARY

THE
FRIENDS OF THE
ORINDA
LIBRARY

Gallery Books   MTV Books

New York   London   Toronto   Sydney   New Delhi

Gallery Books   MTV Books
An Imprint of Simon & Schuster, Inc.
1230 Avenue of the Americas
New York, NY 10020

US (a.) is a work of poetry/fiction and historical fiction. Apart from the well-known actual people, events, and locales that figure in the narrative, all names, places, and incidents are the products of the author's imagination or are used fictitiously. Any resemblance to current events or locales, or to living persons, is entirely coincidental.

First MTV Books/Gallery Books trade paperback edition September 2015

GALLERY BOOKS and colophon are registered trademarks of Simon & Schuster, Inc.

For information about special discounts for bulk purchases, please contact Simon & Schuster Special Sales at 1-866-506-1949 or business@simonandschuster.com.

The Simon & Schuster Speakers Bureau can bring authors to your live event. For more information or to book an event, contact the Simon & Schuster Speakers Bureau at 1-866-248-3049 or visit our website at www.simonspeakers.com.

Interior design by Davina Mock-Maniscalco

Cover art © Angelbert Metoyer

Manufactured in the United States of America

10   9   8   7   6   5   4   3   2   1

Library of Congress Cataloging-in-Publication Data is available.

ISBN 978-1-4767-7932-4
ISBN 978-1-4767-7933-1 (ebook)

Permissions appear on page 257 and should be considered an extension of this copyright page.

Dedicated to America Williams

. . . in a blackness so complete
that the mind rebelled against it.

—Arthur C. Clarke

Foreword

"I'm a NGH too," said the aboriginal kid in Redfern, as me and CX inspected his grafitti. "What's up, my NGH," said that Palestinian kid in Jerusalem. "Peace, NGH," said the French boy on the Metro. There was the Sierra Leonian–German rapper who asked if I had any influence over other American rappers, because when Wu-Tang finished telling the audience, "I love y'all. Y'all my niggas," the audience took it to heart and started saying it to each other and to the non-American blacks that lived amongst them. It went viral. In South Africa, they never asked me about the usage of the word "nigga"—it was always more about why there were so many rappers giving so much love to diamonds. "Don't they know the ramifications in places like here and Sierra Leone where we mine them?" "Ain't nobody thinkin 'bout that," I would say. "Mothafuckas is caught up!" I had a little more swag in my speak in places like Soweto. Real recognize real and performs its greatest gesture. I was at home. But I sometimes visited places where no one of my complexion had ever been seen, where I sometimes had the opportunity to be somebody's first. I remember Karlovy Vary: I arrived in a stone village, between mountains on a train from Munich. The day before I had visited the concentration camp in Dachau where, if memory serves, I was the only one there. I had no visible witness. Yet here, the people stared as if they had never seen anyone like me, except maybe on TV. Having no real sense of decorum, they stared with mouths agape. I was staring, too. It had only been five years since they had become an independent state. Western goods were just beginning to flood the market. Girls wobbled in high heels and cheap fitted jeans. The nightclubs played music that had until recently been banned. I remember dancing at like 4 AM to Prince's "Pussy Control" in a riotous club called Hell, amazed that everyone knew the words. It was my first club experience where, literally, everyone in the place was dancing. Earlier that day, I walked through a narrow street when a little girl, maybe four or five, holding her mother's hand, lit up when she saw me. Her mother, busy observing something in a shopwindow, felt her daughter's urgent tug and followed her eyes to mine. Maybe I expected the mother to admonish the kid with the typical, "Don't point." Instead, her eyes widened as she picked up her daughter, never taking her eyes off mine, and she approached. With her daughter held out in front of her—the little outstretched hands—was like a medieval painting approaching on a dolly. The closer they got, the more the inquisitive wonder turned into a smile. With hands no more than a few inches from my face, the mother managed a meager, "Please." I stood still. Looking into their eyes as they beheld me, the brush of small fingers against my face. The mother's smile was careful in how she chose to savor the moment. . . . Her eyes watered as she mouthed, "Thank you" and then quickly hustled her daughter away. What else could I do but wonder . . . and wander? Yet, I never considered myself having truly visited a place without entering someone's kitchen. In Belize, I had traveled amongst the Garifuna with no money. The Rastas amongst them kept me fed and always offered a spot where I could lay my sleeping bag on their floor. The Tamil in southern India just assumed I was Sri Lankan. In Paris, their great love affair had been with black American culture. I discussed politics, drank wine, hung out in Cameroonian dives, and made frequent trips to the farmer's market.

I moved from Los Angeles to Paris, with my thirteen-year-old, in the spring of 2009. Voted for "change" and skipped town soon after. Wanted to peep it from the outside. America had so much to do with perception. Obama's election was a global celebration. I remember arriving in Marrakesh during the primaries and the taxi driver from the airport was gleaming after I told him I was from the U.S. "Obama!" he said. "*Inchallah*, Obama!" After years of traveling, and studying abroad as a teenager, I was enamored by people's perception of America. How they saw us. And my "us" was particular. In some places, they had never encountered a black American, yet they had surely heard of *us*. "Martyr Loser King!" was what I heard through their thick accents. "Nina Simone," "Michael Jackson," "Tyson, Jordan, take your pick . . ."

My daughter had the ominous experience of being in her eighth grade class at College Valmy, with about thirty other recent immigrants, when one of her classmates' phone rang in the classroom. Typical no-no. The student, a thirteen-year-old Afghani boy saw the number and, without hesitation, answered. He spoke quickly, was quiet a moment, before he burst into tears and ran out the room. Another Afghani boy in the class stood and chased after him, stopping first to give the teacher a rushed explanation, while the students looked on in shock and confusion. The teacher looked at my daughter and said, "Your country kill his mother." Not the response I expected, stashing my hash in its regular hiding place and belting out, "How was school today?" She said she sat with him at lunch and told him, "I'm not that kind of American."

But here we were, now, back in America. The New York I'd abandoned fourteen years earlier had changed considerably. I'd visit my old haunts in Brooklyn or Greenwich Village, notice the pedestrians standing on the curb waiting for the light to change as I skipped between cars, thinking, "Where the fuck are the New Yorkers?" It seemed as if the city had been turned over to NYU students and bankers. I'd flash on the images of the Occupy movement, which I had studied from abroad, thinking, "So that's it? Did the 1% win?" But despite the conundrum of finding affordable housing, where it was proven that the answer to my question was a simple and definitive *yes*, New York was being kind to me. Here I was being commissioned by my publisher to write a book of poetry. My earlier works had all been ideas and manuscripts that I had proposed to them, but this time was different. They knew what they wanted me to write about: America. They imagined it impossible to assert that nothing had changed. The election of Obama symbolized the beginning of a new era. An era that I had

3

deliberately observed from the outside, and now was my turn to name it. Of course, the proposition was not exactly out of the blue. They were also proposing this after having turned down my most recent manuscript, a graphic novel. I had begun imagining the story of a hacker living in Burundi near the border of the Congo.

He grows up on a hill where, one day, purveyors discover coltan. The hill becomes a mine. He's given the option of working or departing. After months of working in the mine, he sets off and wanders until he arrives in a burnt-out prairie of motherboards, wires, scraps, and monitors: an e-waste camp. The hacker, who actually isn't a hacker yet, scavenges enough parts to build a wall, another wall, a roof, and lives in a shack built of old computer parts, with one question: How do u turn this thing on?

He dreams of an old wanderer that passed through his village as a child, who told him the secret of how to see the white dwarf with the naked eye, how to predict the flooding of the Nile. The binary equation the old man had used as proof of his origin, and the realization that he had grown up sleeping on the metal that now powers the future, would count as his explanation of how he innately understood how to code.

There's something about this boy, like the Eden Abez song that Nat King Cole made famous. Our hero, this strange, enchanted boy, travels very far, very far, over land, away from the now heavily patrolled mine to a place where he attracts other young scavengers, refugees, pariah, escapees, runaways, orphans. One night, a few of them are eating and joking about their lot in life. They know they are not rich, but they also know that they have something and they decide to name it. *Losers*. They call themselves losers with pride. Perhaps it's just about belonging. They determine that to be a loser is like the modern sense of being a sinner. They also come up with a new name for God: Motherboard.

4

Sinners vs. Losers

Well, it's the sinners vs. the losers
and the losers win every time

because the losers fight the system
while the sinners lost in their minds.

And if the losers are the winners
then the winners are losers too.

because the losers fight for justice
while the winners lost in their truth.

Lost in their truth.
Lost in their truth.

2xs

He powers his computer and discovers the world: maps, movies, music, encyclopedias and dictionaries, digital compasses, news feeds and fashion. One night, they venture into town for a drink at a local bar called "Hell" and he meets a beautiful . . . well, at first, he's not sure if it's a girl or boy, and he doesn't think it matters. Later, when they talk, she tells him, "I am a modem." And that's exactly who she is: Neptune Frost. When she returns to his makeshift cabin, she stares at the wall of monitors and recognizes a face drawn on a screen. "Martyr Loser King," she says.

BY THE TIME of my meeting with my publisher, I'd already demoed an album with the character, MartyrLoserKing, in mind. It was a multimedia project: an album, a graphic novel, and a play. The reason for the play was simple: I missed theater, and instead of going on tour with a concept album, I thought it would be cooler to stay put, dress the set, and perform the songs in the context of the story: a musical. I had already found producers for the play and a label to help me finance the production of the album. New York, which like I said was being very kind to me, was the perfect place to put this play on its feet. My publisher may have turned down the graphic novel component of the project, but this new proposal would be just one more thing for me to think of, and arguably something I'd be thinking of naturally: What was it like to be back in America?

A few months earlier, after about thirty tries, I found a place and settled in Harlem. Most of the landlords I encountered in Brooklyn, quite frankly, didn't trust an artist's fluctuant income. Harlem was perfect and turned out to be what I missed the most. I wandered the halls of the Jumel Mansion listening to *Birth of the Cool*. I traced the footsteps of Dizzy, Bird, Nina, Ellison, Baldwin, Ellington, Billie, Langston. I had given myself a month to work on another project I had begun conceptualizing while in Paris: a work of historical fiction in the form of a screenplay based on the love story between Miles Davis and Juliette Greco. The story would begin with Miles at the Hotel America in Harlem, just after he had returned from meeting Juliette on his first trip to Paris. Lovesick, lonely, confused, he resorts to heroin. It's not just Juliette—it's the taste of freedom and the realization that it didn't taste the same on these shores. In a month's time, he'd gone from debating with Sartre, drinking with Picasso, making love to Juliette, and returning to a land where the love he had just experienced was against the law. He becomes a junkie and spends his days watching tap dancers battle. His father gets word of what his son is up to in New York and brings him to his ranch in Arkansas to kick the habit. There, Miles goes cold turkey and begins an incongruent dream of his time with Juliette: L'Héroïne.

I spent considerable time interviewing Juliette Greco while in Paris. *"What do you know about dating a white woman?"* she purred over her chardonnay at the Hotel Lutecia. Part of what had interested me about Miles's time in Paris was what he had unwittingly landed into the middle of: Saint-Germain-des-Prés 1949. Boris Vian, Miles's host, who had the honor of making the introduction to his "little sister" Juliette, was in the middle of the highly publicized court case against his

6

book, *I Spit On Your Grave*, which the Cartel d'Action Sociale et Morale had denounced, particularly after a gruesome murder had happened in a Paris hotel, where a man had strangled his mistress and left the book open, bedside, next to the corpse, with a sentence underlined, "I again felt that strange sensation that ran up my back as my hand closed on her throat and I couldn't stop myself; it came; it was so strong that I let her go . . ."

One of the interesting points in the case was that Boris was being tried for translating "objectionable material," when in fact, Vernon Sullivan, the black American author he had claimed to discover, was in fact himself. Boris played trumpet, sang, and had helped arrange to bring the Miles Davis Quintet to the Paris Festival International de Jazz, which would count as Miles's first time out of the country, and more importantly, his first as a frontman, no longer under the shadow of Charlie Parker. Juliette had just begun shooting the poetic narrative, *Orpheus*, with Cocteau. Sartre had just completed his analysis of the Negritude movement in his essay "Orphee Negre" in the Foreword of the *Anthologie de la nouvelle poésie nègre et malgache*, compiled by Léopold Senghor, future president of Senegal, and included Almee Cesalre and the fiery poetry of black francophone intellectuals rejecting French colonialism, and in walks Miles. Sartre asks Miles, "Why don't you marry Juliette?" The two couldn't keep their hands off each other. The eighty-three-year-old Juliette bites her lip when she talks about it. I imagine Sartre as the friar in a fantastic rendition of "Miles and Juliette." Black American Montagues and French-bohemian Capulets.

"Because I love her too much," Miles explains to Sartre. He couldn't bear the weight of how their very open romance would be received back in New York and in the States. Years later, Miles visited Juliette in her suite at the Waldorf Astoria and left in a fury after the hotel's maître d' threw their food on the floor after seeing she and Miles alone in the room. He called her later that night and said, "I don't ever want to see you again here, in a country where this kind of relationship is impossible." That episode had happened in 1957, almost ten years after their initial meeting.

That was almost sixty years ago, I think as I pass a group of black and brown teenagers being stopped and frisked at the exit of the D train on 145th and St. Nicholas. Harlem reminds me of Barbès, the African-populated district in Paris where I'd go when I needed some of that down-home spice in my food. It's January, a month since I signed the contract to write the book of poems with my newfound impressions of the U.S. The meteorologists are throwing around terms like "polar vortex." I'm heading to the studio to mix my wife's first feature, which I'm scoring and musical supervising. An underground portrait of America, haunted, hollow, and pure. Shot in thirty-two states, it was her first extensive journey across the continent and country. For me, it was an opportunity to see America through the eyes of a stranger. She fell in love with New Orleans, was tickled to death by Dallas, took a picture of a sign at a gas station in Idaho that said anyone wearing a cross would receive a ten-percent discount. "This is America!" I told her. She couldn't believe how many flags and crosses were visible from the highway. "Yep. What can I say?" I found myself repeating. What can I say?

The music keeps creeping up in me. It's a fairly regulated ecosystem. The reading inspires the writing, the writing is shaped through music, the music peaks and inspires a sonic idea, and then some. From keyboard to keyboard, I vacillate. A poet—Imamu Amiri Baraka—dies and I'm asked to speak at his funeral. I come across this passage:

> A typewriter?—why shd it only make use of the tips of the fingers as contact points of flowing multi directional creativity. If I invented a word placing machine, an "expression-scriber," *if you will*, then I would have a kind of instrument into which I could step and sit or sprawl or hang and use not only my fingers to make words express feelings but elbows, feet, head, behind, and all the sounds I wanted, screams, grunts, taps, itches, I'd have magnetically recorded, at the same time, and translated into word—or perhaps even the final xpressed thought/feeling wd not be merely word or sheet, but *itself*, the xpression, three dimensional—able to be touched, or tasted or felt, or entered, or heard or carried like a speaking singing constantly communicating charm. *A typewriter is corny!!*

WHEN I ARRIVE at the funeral, I'm amazed by the huge, building-sized American flag hanging from the extended ladder of a fire engine on the blocked off street where the service is taking place. The building is packed with activists, freedom fighters, social workers, Marxists, Muslims, musicians, artists, teachers, national/international dignitaries, and a marching police band with bagpipes and drums. I feel myself being sucked into a vortex. Later I'm forced to transcribe from a recording what I recited beside the coffin. I'm surprised to hear myself say, "This is a stickup."

I get an email asking if I'd like to audition for a Broadway musical directed by Kenny Leon. The play features the work of Tupac Shakur. I read about the production in Paris soon after his hologram appeared at a music festival and didn't think it was a good idea. I read the script and begin to consider it. The Christian undertones concern me, but the opening lines of the play, taken from the song "My Block," win me every time.

I'M ZONING ON Pac. Something comes over me. Initially, I told my wife I want to land the role just to turn it down. Over the week of preparation, I feel myself beginning to catch feelings. I start to question how I'll cope if I don't get the part. When I arrive at the audition, I see a well-known actor and think, *but of course.* The piano player leans into it and so do I. I forget words and begin to freestyle. If there's one thing I know how to do, it's rap and act. Wait, that's two. Kenny Leon, who I was excited to meet, sits ice-cold behind the table. No smile. No sign of being impressed. He is swaying to the beat 'tho. Music is like that.

I leave the audition and pass by the office of my old acting manager. I figure maybe I should be reconnecting with representation, do some more auditions, whatever. I stop by the office unannounced, as I used to when I lived in New York years ago. The guard at the door calls upstairs to see if it's okay. He shakes his head as he hangs up the phone. "Sorry." I buy a lottery ticket before I get home. I feel weird, somewhat depressed. I arrive home to an email asking if I can do a final callback on Monday. That Tuesday morning, they call me bright and early. Fuck. Another project. This one's a job. I have a few shows to do with a jazz musician in Europe before I come back and start rehearsals. New York is whirlwind, a polar vortex.

The jazz musician asks me to send five or six poems for him to compose pieces, which we'll perform with his quintet at the Cully Jazz Festival in Switzerland. This is my first time looking over the poems I've begun writing since I've been home. He sends me back heavily notated music sheets with my words between the bars. At the rehearsal, he tells me he saw me read at the poet's funeral. The band begins, my world spins.

When rehearsals for the play commence, the wheels and machinery of Broadway are already in motion. Here is an essence of this city and nation. The island of Manhattan is that to me. A war of energy and definitions. A machine in perfect harmony against and despite itself. The Lower East Side's feelings about Wall Street are on the walls. Wall Street buys the walls and repaints them. Ain't nobody fucking with Chinatown. The rumors say Harlem is next to go, but something convinces me it will keep its rich, dark center.

I'm reading Robert Moses and Columbus. I had started reading Columbus in Paris after picking it up at Shakespeare and Company. Somehow I had missed the fact that this mthrfckr kept a journal. Man, that shit is extraordinary. You can see the root of the whole equation. The descriptions of the people he encountered hold their own magic. I spend a night cocktailing Fredo Santana flow with Columbus text. Robert Moses is another one. He discovered how to always get his way. He wasn't the first, of course. Every night I'm repeating

> Cops give a damn about a negro.
> Pull a trigger/kill a nigga
> He's a hero.

ONCE THE PLAY begins, I'm no longer singularly focused. I'm painting, writing, turned my dressing room into a little studio. I'm making music. Fired up. I'm thinking of the indigenous that saw this island as a sight for hunting and ritual. I read a passage in a book that says that when the Spanish got to the mainland of South America, the disease spread at such a rate that the Incas were dying of influenza long before they ever saw a European, that the men who described them took little note of the fact that they had recently been ravaged by plague

10

and disease. By the time settlers arrive in the 1600s, more than 90% of the population is dead. I dream of Evelyn Nesbit and the red velvet swing. I learn Bert Williams performed on this same stage in 1919. The performance. The ritual. I'm a candle.

Lights flicker and the play is over. The producer lost his investment. They say it was too political. They say he should have gone to regional theater first. In my mind, the violence that the play depicted was exactly that—regional American theater now ready for the main stage and national discussion. I write an open letter for the press on closing night and then decide against sharing it. I hop on a plane for a writer's residency at the Banff Centre in Canada. More America from the outside. While I'm there, a friend asks if I'm seeing a bunch of shit on my timeline about Ferguson, Missouri. I log in/zone out. It's a blood moon. I reread what I had hesitated to share just a few days before.

> What did you expect? That critics would rave in the face of raving audiences? That each one would not have the seemingly independent idea of living up to their title? That they would realize when they are playing into the hands of those that wish to see us disappear, to mute our voices, who've heard enough hollering and murdered it for fear of hearing? It's too easy to say that a play about the lives of incarcerated black men in America is generic. Institutionalized racism in America is generic (which is a fucking shame when you know that "race," itself, is a social construct. The mthrfckr don't even exist). It's fascinating that one would find a play about ending gun violence in an unnamed midwestern American city, generic. Is it because we read about said violence (ultraviolence) in the better-read sections of the papers for which they write? We hold these truths to be self-evident. We know the story. We know the type.
>
> Imagine this a monologue. The darkened stage upholds the mere silhouette of a man, twenty feet above the ground, addressing the audience. Imagine the audience: a keyboard before the screen.

Is the man looking from the screen or toward it? Is he mouthing words to himself, or typing? Tapping the heads of the audience with his fingertips . . . space bar: the orchestra . . .

You choose the music. The message is the same. Cut the bullshit. Not the critique. Nobody gives a fuck about that shit. Cut the systematic silencing of diversity. Cut the ties that bind us to pathological denial of experience for the taste of sameness. You make entertainment bland. I like a little truth in my blunt. Face it, I'm real.

Real NGHs in real plays. Does that frighten you? That I typed the n-word? Imagine the fear! Imagine the fear! I'm just playing. I'll describe it as a love story.

What do you love about theater? What I love is the invitation to gaze into an unseen world, peopled like our own. To find pieces of my story in their story. To feel, to laugh, to learn. I know you only like party rap. Ain't nuthin' but a gangsta party. You know you been dying to dance with my hologram . . .

Holler if you ain't scared of the beat.

I bet you think I'm angry. What could I do to demand a deeper observation? Would you like to feel my bullet wounds? In terms of bullet wounds, they're rather generic but particular to the touch. Oh, you play rough. I play dangerously close to allegations. You like your Ali's more like Rocky. Ali went to jail for not fighting. But I'm through with prison and the overplayed trappings of your system.

When I asked Harry Belafonte his views after seeing our play, he said, "You have taken an Afri-centric story and placed it on a Eurocentric stage. The fight you are fighting is larger than you think." Think again.

FUCK. NOW, I'M here. Angry. And I realize now that that was why I left this place. Not because I couldn't overcome it. I always had. Never personal. It came with the territory. Easily justified. Never had the privilege of oblivion. Born into something that was ongoing and brutal in its hypocrisy. I simply wanted to experience, if only momentarily, a life free from it.

In France, I recorded an album called *Volcanic Sunlight,* challenging myself to write songs without anger. In my daily life I was hardly angry. Music became the place where I stored and channeled it all. There was no question of edge. I wanted the drums and instruments to speak for me. I wanted to float.

I had been dreaming of Atlantis for over a decade. An island with a mountain in its middle. The walls of a city built up and around the mountain. The first pyramid. The mountain erupts up and over the walls of the city. The quake of the eruption submerges the island under water. The sulphur seals and preserves the walls. The inhabitants adapt. On land, they are forgotten. After thirteen generations, they sense a shift in the traffic overhead. The tormented energy of the cargo. The whales' choice of song. Their engineers devise a method of sending messages through water downloaded through the dreams of the people bound as cargo. Some speak of those who made it to these shores as survivors. In Atlantis, the ones who survived are the ones who were thrown overboard. A molten sun, deep beneath the ocean floor, shines up and through them. My dreams are no escape, but they begin again.

Deeper still, beneath the anger, is a depression, a wound. Earth's recessive gene. Come on, son. Snap out of it. It ain't like that. Truths are truths, that's fair. But we change truth. Reality based upon agreement. Begging to differ. Every reason to be mad at the game. The game isn't fair by nature. Only one team can win. Only the loser fights for a tie. Then it becomes a question of changing the game. Mastery. And you're mastering a few things at once: timing; originality . . . confidence alone won't get you over. It'll take more than one act of humility. You may have to be broken. No one wishes for it. Other things are given. The connection between the given and the earned is not to be confused with earnings from the given. Your success will be based upon the organization of your thoughts and actions, on the categorization of your epiphanies with proofs and analysis. This is not something that can be imposed upon you. It is in your best interest because you are free.

Whole passages of text begin to stream through me. I make no sense of it.

I'm in the streets. In conversations in cafés. Late night discussions at home. The governors are calling for calm. The president is calling for peace. The police are calling for obedience. The protesters are calling for justice. The media is calling them violent. The police are calling them animals. The foreigners are calling them persecuted. The locals are joining the call. But then, I'm in Harlem.

Once again.
Once again.
Once again.

Standing at the threshold of birth, breath, and afterthought.

There is no right answer, but there is something that is: Love is. Growth is. Death is. And Transcendence.

Swirling up from heavy downward upward colossus, collision . . .

I have outgrown this song.

The things that once moved me
have kept me in my place.

Miles Davis in your face!

"Bitches brew," he said, failing to see the context. "They ain't loyal." He had no reference to the album or even Miles Davis, beyond a simple face/horn recognition. As an American, he was a product. His lack of vision, manufactured. Objectified that which he silently worshipped. Measured the actions of

women against his own privilege and power, remain-
ing oblivious of the transaction. Sold his abilities for
possibilities of comfort. Saw no need to question the
network/system, simply because it worked for him.

We call that selfish here.
Time has no boundaries, here.
Attention, a utility, here.
We pay, like water.

Built of defense.

Not to say
we are strong.

Fortified.

The iron and metals
that sprang from us.

Each mountain
a university.

Dictated by land
Sun
current
Earth is not democratic.

Thought is second to air in its capacity.

HOW ARE THE protesters behaving? The protesters are sitting on toilets, picking up their kids from school, on their way home from work, grading papers, fixing shoes, selling beers, drinking them, just got out of dance class at their after-school program, are out fetching water from the well, using fruity loops to make beats, eating cereal, stretching goat skin over hollowed pieces of wood, pulling their masks from their backpacks, applying eyeliner, tagging signs, swiping phones, typing into their computers, sharing/blocking their locations . . . They are not hard to find.

As a poet whose creative meanderings have sometimes been short-circuited/hardwired by political realisms, whose open eyes have forbidden me the privilege of not seeing the blatant and the obvious, who is bored by the slow-crawl of progress, disillusioned by media, art, representation and the cultural development of "taste," who must be taught, teach, and point out what could easily be empathized, who must sit at a dinner table listening to his children become politicized and angry by the mindless blurts of their peers and teachers, who is forced to defend slogans that should go without saying, slogans I cannot bring myself to type, who thinks the fight is surely beyond the petty/profound travails of racial injustice and should be pointed more heartedly towards a discussion on class and entitlement, except that we ain't there yet, who knows how race was used to divide and control the poor by those who would rather give to poor whites an unjustifiable yet easily manipulated sense of entitlement than money, who knows a social construct when she sees one, who must face that the expression "every new poem is a revision of the last" is not always because the poet seeks clearer ways of stating things but also because society is fixed in its blind spots, who flashes back on his mother in '63, applauds images from Ferguson and attempts to re-create them in New York streets, who can't breathe except that I am, I am nothing if not *verklempt*. Dead. I can't.

Hackers seem better fit to do the dirty work. They give it to us plain. In the last decade, they have released enough private and classified information to bring millions of protesters to the streets to overthrow corrupt governments, demand changes, to make executives apologize, while the privileged and powerful seem so lost in their privatized bubbles that they can do no more than incriminate themselves. But then, heroes disappoint. Leaders disappoint. Nations disappoint. Power corrupts. Privilege blinds. The promise of transparency requires purification rituals. Sharing every thought would essentially be less than thoughtful. The inclusion of fears, doubts, and other checked ululations would undoubtedly lead thinkers astray. And what of material goods? A surplus at some point would betray the secret. You are overcharging or underpaying. Calculate my worth and sell me. There are other systems at play. The use of law to regulate the system displays the absolute: there are many ways to win. Play by the rules and discover what they ignored or didn't notice. Change the game; now this is footwork, the music and the dance will win. The secret of music. Playing by the rules means not breaking them. If we don't break the rules, we perpetuate the pattern. Legislate new rules by addressing its proven shortcomings. You will need a majority vote and a whole heap of patience, but may cut time with a charismatic speaker. Identify with so-called minority. Realize when majority of minority works to defend an even smaller "calculated" minority. Inspire collectivity. Change terms. Make minimum wage living wage. Small shifts may be the light switch. Change names like Puffy. Change behavioral perception. Look out!

THE INFORMATION AGE means your information, too. Distortion of the truth for hits. The ol' hits vs. likes argument. The celebrity verification ritual. The Supremes court. The "this is my opinion, which is based on facts" routine, the faux news sites disguised as white-collar criminology experts, the movies with revolving casts, Christian Bale as everything under the sun. Wind-up puppets of the universe attack the caliphate. The surfers are like, "whoa." Guy Fawkes condoms in a Swiss bank vault. Calls that pussy ISIS. These Mthrfckrs don't want to back down.The unanimous gold mine shapes and envelops us. We are what we think we are. We believe we are white trash and cling to it. We puff our chests. We believe we are black, Jewish and, by persecution, chosen, singled out. We form tighter bonds. We are what we say we are and will not be defeated except when exploited by those who control the mine. Who place value on its contents. My perception is mine. The mind is a minefield or a gold mine. What was the viewership on the night the mines erupted? How much to charge for the monthly subscribership to tune in?

What can I plug my unit into? You are now plugged into mine. What is the value of our precious resource? Pay attention. Ask them, go ahead. The cost of one black life is the establishment.

I AM BLACK, I say. I am American, I say. I am Indian, I say. I am white, I say. I am Asian. I am trans. I am female. "I belong to that group," I say. "So watch what you say!" That group is an extension of family. I belong to that family. I was born into that family. When it becomes my turn to criticize my family, I am nineteen, home for Thanksgiving. I am ten years old at the same Thanksgiving table questioning why we are celebrating the slaughter of the indigenous. I am thirty, I am forty and done with my critique. I have given in. I'm at the head of the table. Shall we pray?

    The state of New Jersey wants Assata as its martyred saint. "No saint!" says enforcement, who have built their case of refurbished southern poplar auctioned direct from Billie's throat. A two-million dollar coffin, nailed shut: solid evidence. Big bang, evolutionary social (theory) network. Black lives mattered. The hashtag, the cross, the poplar tree.

The church as the original start-up.

Branding and Its Origins by Pope Gregory IV, Constantinople Press.

Martyrs: the other 1%.

TONIGHT I WAS grabbed by a police officer. I caught a glimpse of his bulk and twisted face as he barged towards me. I had been lying on the sidewalk beside my wife and a group of maybe two hundred others. We marched protesting the grand jury's decision to not indict another overly brutal police officer. This one had strangled a man selling loose cigarettes on the sidewalk with an illegal choke hold while the man said and repeated eleven times, "I can't breathe."

Just before becoming a parent, I stumble upon poetry as a means of weaving my disparate thoughts, meanderings, love of language, philosophy, and suddenly I am writing spells. Spells to equip my children with tools and fortification for the fight that is come, a fight that I had tried to convince myself would not come. A fight that could be overcome with thought, words, music, a collage of evolutionary shifts that might explain how one generation goes from being colored to black, and another that infuses "nigger" with love. But still, I am unprepared.

Photo ops with the family of the victims.

Introduction

This is my mother. Is there a trace of anger or fear on her face? Does she inhabit any physical trait of doubt in her cause? Is she holding a weapon in her purse? What are the officers thinking? What do *their* children think when they see this photo? Do they see their parents' cause as just or simply see them as "doing their jobs" "upholding the law" "people of their times"? Is it possible to detach bloodlines from historical allegiance? Which came first, the protest or the law? What is she singing? These are the questions that circle my head. This picture, without meme, will trace memory. A memory that I will inherit.

Scientists argue. Then come genetics. More arguing, more theories. Sips tea, I type. I've got the perfect caption. Blast thoughts and reap reactions. Little time for reasoning. My mother now living alone in a city she inherited from my sisters, shows little interest in her memory. Runs to keep up with the present. Shares articles about corruption and fraud, good news for believers. Not one to blind-copy.

Never saw this photo until last year when my cousin found it on eBay. "Isn't this Aunt Juanita?" Yep. "The photo was on the front page of *The New York Herald Tribune*," my father had boasted through the years, though they never kept a copy. It was never her claim to fame. Hers is an honest to goodness American story. The granddaughter of hardworking Haitian immigrants who arrived on Ellis Island in 1917. She was born and raised between Amityville, Long Island and East New York, Brooklyn. The oldest of nine, she was expected to quit school and get a job when she was sixteen, but her stepfather fought off the hounds and supported her in realizing her dream: studying children's education at Brooklyn College. While still at a teacher's assistant at The Little Red School House in Greenwich Village, she was invited to a party by her Alpha Kappa Alpha sorority sister and met my father, a young seminarian en route to being called to pastor his first church.

Teachers and preachers, that's a classic combination. Alongside my father, she marched, she prayed, she taught Sunday school, and emphasized black history way before the public school system adopted it. Along with birthing three children of her own, me being the youngest, she had many children who adopted her in her thirty-plus years of teaching. Always enthusiastically adventurous, my mom drove my two older sisters and me through thirty-five states one summer. She wanted us to see it all, not just the images in the encyclopedias and textbooks, but the real Petrified Forest, the Mojave, the Grand Canyon, the Gulf of Mexico, the horse ranges of Oklahoma, the lights of Las Vegas, the hills of San Francisco, Universal Studios. We slept in the car, ate bologna sandwiches, and camped outside of Western Unions when the money got tight. And with her enthusiasm for travel and learning, my older sisters and I all set off to be exchange students. Besides, we were growing up in Newburgh, New York, and with its vibrant schools and violent streets we had little else to do but dream of getting away.

When I arrived in the southern state of Paraná, Brazil, at sixteen, my first shock was to learn that I was to go to night school. In this rural southern town, kids in high school were expected to work the fields during the day. The second shock came with the news that the teachers were on strike, and for the next four months, there would be no school. By the time classes began, I had already learned the language, thanks to the time I spent translating Sade, Public Enemy, and lessons from my host mother and brother. I had also befriended the school's English teacher, who served as one of my host-brother's capoeira instructors. By the time school began I was no longer expected to go, but invited to visit, on

22

occasion, as the English teacher's assistant. Every time I showed up, everything stopped, other teachers and classes would gather to ask dozens of questions. The main two: "Is America really free?" echoed by ". . . like in the movies?" and then, "What's it like to be sprayed by a fire hose?" I'd usually explain it away as if it were a sex tape my parents made before my conception: an embarrassment that predated my existence. I had other things to ponder as I followed the maid around the house trying to find ways to spark the coversation that would lead her to invite me home with her. In her mind, it seemed, to be American meant I was rich, where to be black, like her, implied poverty. The big rumor was that the Brazilian soccer star Pele had become rich and was now considered white. I'd watch his girlfriend Xuxa on TV every morning, though I really had a thing for Maravilha.

I'd walk into stores and the salesperson would normally flick their wrist and make an attempt to "sssssss" me away. I'd respond in a loud and proper, "Excuse me?" and suddenly everything would change. I'd be invited out for a drink or to their home for dinner. I tried my luck for an entire month after meeting a fellow exchange student/adventurer from Belgium. We traveled by bus from city to city. We'd arrive in a town mid-afternoon, find the local mall, let people realize we were foreign, get fed, get taken out to a club, then back to the bus station where we'd choose another city, four to eight hours away, spread out on the backseats of the bus, and arrive in the next city, ready to do it again. And it never failed.

When I returned to the the States, the local paper decided to interview me about my time abroad. I attempted to explain my amazement at the interest in and influence of U.S. culture and capital; how curious the kids were; how I had visited supermarkets, saw groceries wrapped in brown paper, like schoolbooks, observed naturally browning fruits and vegetables, learning of the global stretch of U.S. corporations and the chemical demands of the FDA in the same breath, "nossos melhores frutas vão para os Estados Unidos." To my discontent, the article's headline read, "Williams Amazed at the Power of the U.S."

Soon after I left for college, my mom dyed her hair blond and, for her fiftieth birthday, bought herself a Jeep. She then announced that she had applied to become an exchange teacher and BOOM, she was off to teach English and math in the Gambia. She would miss my college graduation, but my graduation gift would be to spend her final month abroad in West Africa with her. I would fly through Dakar, Senegal, to Banjul where I would spend time with her and the small delegation of African-American teachers she traveled and lived with before venturing by train to back to Senegal and then to Mali. I purchased my first journal for the voyage, something I had been encouraged to do years earlier for Brazil, but could never bring myself to the task. My intital impression when I landed in Senegal was looking out the window of the plane and seeing what seemed to be a policeman and a male civilian, walking, laughing, and holding hands. I kept trying to figure out whether the man was under arrest. Within a few minutes, I noticed another couple, men, holding hands and talking. Questions swirled in my head. In the Gambia, it was the same. Men held hands, boys in my mother's school sat on each other's laps. I reflected on America, my own socialization. I realized, clearly and at once, what I had been taught and what may have been unlearned. The sights, the people, the smells, the tastes, the music, the fashion, the food, the conversations . . . In Senegal, no one would believe I wasn't Senegalese. My mom had learned all the proper Wolof greetings, but me, having just arrived, didn't fare as well. When someone greeted me with "Nanga def," instead of the response my English had garnered in Brazil, here I was met with an incredulous sucking of teeth, as if to say, *Stop bullshitting. You spent a week in New York and now you want to act like you don't remember your language.*

The train ride to Mali was epic. My mom splurged and bought second-class tickets. The seats were metal benches. I sat with other passengers' knees between mine. Chew sticks and bags of dried meat in abundance. The train slowed in remote villages where people would cluster outside of the open windows with bread, fruits, local snacks, and bissop in little plastic Ziploc bags on their heads. I bought an indigo scarf and wrapped it around my head like a Tuareg. I fell in love with its color and smell. I made friends with two kids my age and played cards in the dining car. At some point during the thirty-six-hour ride, my mother told me she had arranged for us to have one of the empty rooms with two beds. I sat across from her as she slept, opened my journal, and began writing my impressions. After a while, I grew tired and looked for the light switch, to turn it off and go to sleep. The light was already off. I walked to the window and the night sky was an indigo blanket wrapped over the moon's shoulders. The stars, like glitter woven into the fabric of the night, were like a million ideas orbiting the mind of the large round face before me. If eyes had been visible I held the space of a pupil. I looked out and saw people sitting in homes, walking through trees and fields. I cued Cassandra Wilson's "Children of the Night" and howled over page. The sun came out and I stood between cars blasting *Illmatic*. People washed clothes in streams, Dogon roamed over on cliffs, as "New York State Of Mind," spun its equation from there to here.

My mom, the perfect tourist, led us through museums, mosques, soccer games, villages where they made mud-cloth . . . We visited artisans, restaurants, and even went to a nightclub together. They played Rakim and I shed a Denzel "Glory" tear on the dance floor. The kids circled around me, possibly because I knew the words or how I suddenly started dancing. Oversized hockey jerseys and Timbs . . . not me, them. And I'm thinking "just steps from Timbuktu . . ." We arrive back in the Gambia, to a general excitement with news of political unrest in the country. The next morning I'm bartering goods my mom had encouraged me to bring—Levi's, high-tops, baseball caps, a deflated basketball . . . American shit for an ancient drum that was, technically, "not for sale," and machine gun fire rings out. People run. Teenagers in soldier uniforms barricade the streets, waving guns, directing traffic as we make our way back to the house and turn on the radio. *"Coup d'état."* The Gambian president has supposedly escaped assassination and is now hiding on an American naval vessel that has mysteriously appeared in the harbor. The broadcaster announces that all international borders have been closed. There are no flights or trains in or out of the country. Foriegners should report to their respective embassies. Americans in our area are supposed to find "safe haven" at the home of the local American ambassador. It is a group of us, nine African-Americans clustered together making our way through empty streets, passing carefully by the young soldiers who pay us no mind, arrive at the residence of the ambassador and a man with a wire behind his ear answers the door seeming sincerely shocked to see us. He snarls, "What do you want?" My mom and an elder teacher of the group inform him that we are American citizens, now trapped in the country, and have heard the broadcast instructions stating that this is where we should come to be fed and find "safe haven." The man looks us up and down and blurts, "Well, if I had known you folks were coming, I'd a pulled the grits out the pantry." That was the first time I ever heard my mom curse somebody out.

But in this picture, she's not cursing. There's not a trace of anger on her face. Without context, one might assume she's doing an interpretive dance. My drum machine beside my computer, my mind is on the music, I am attempting to score the moment. A moog sub-phatty synth and a vintage Yamaha ex5 sequencer behind me, I am in the cockpit of a small craft hovering just above the police van. The year is 1963, 2015, 1976, 1994, 2063 and that is the problem. The dance is the time machine. The dervish swipes the pose. The land is the motherboard, oh Vortex. The music feeds the wire. My mother, swirling beneath me, lands in the police officers' arms. They lift her up and place her, ceremoniously, into the paddy wagon. The security footage shows the dancers in seated prose. The audience, twitching in front of their screens, shift in their seats. A perfomance that has been repeated enough for it to have become tradition. DISRUPTION. I am the circuit-breaker. The Parralel's choreographer has helped me orchestrate my movement, yet I fear I have missed my cue. Earth has become a series of reenactments. This show "America" is for performative history buffs. I am a pirate signal, the crack in your phone as you lift it from the pavement. The vibration of the bass opens the lower hatch, short-circuits the performative world below as I extend my hand and lift my mother up and through. She crosses the threshold as the beat drops. She settles in the passenger seat beside me and I flash on driving with my permit as a teenager. The look on her face is that of a ballerina dungeoned in a theater and let out for *Swan Lake* performances, who one day, after an infinite cycle, exits her cell and finds herself thrust into another production. New music, story, and background. My mother adjusts her body in the seat and turns in my direction. As if we were mid-coversation, she begins to tell me the story of how she found me in the backyard as a toddler, banging a branch . . . "You found me?!" I say. She gives a sarcastic humph. "Yes, Stacey, I found you," before continuing, "you were holding a tree branch, like a staff, banging a rhythm on the ground and chanting something, repeatedly . . ."

THERE IS NO photograph or reenactment for me. My memory of this experience will begin as a story I was told, but with time it will render images, video. For now, I am listener, as my mother imagines me chanting some ancestral language while banging her ceremonious stick. I am under her spell. It is not in my power to disprove or disapprove of my mother's imagination. My mother fought for her dream. And I am in it.

Prologue

Suddenly it's all too much. Everything is immediate. We can share thoughts at the rate of thought. Images. Music. Everything is available. Suddenly we had it all in our pocket. Suddenly we could see people as we spoke to them, on our phones, on our computers. Suddenly we were all connected. Wars persisted, genocides, famines, gang rapes, financial blunders, crashes, all that had dominated when headlines were headlines. Gross atrocities shared common space with blogs on shoes, trends in plastic surgery, reports on how long the wait was outside the movie theater, rants on pet peeves, and baby photos. It was as if every thought, every idea decided to be heard at once. And when the words and images were reflected back from virtual worlds with countless viewers and comments, a narcissistic pride took hold. Look what I wrote. How many hits, how many likes, how many follows. And I decidedly joined the party. The uninformed didn't suddenly inform themselves. The world, it turned out, was not entirely studious. Though many studied trends, exchanged recipes, ideas, political analysis, searched for turn-ons and laughs, it was evident that the sources chosen for information retrieval were still boundaried by personal tastes, interests, and prejudices, and one could easily continue to exist within the idea that their way of seeing the world was *the* way of seeing the world. Arguments about privilege, the advantages of the rich and connected, were becoming troublingly obsolete. People with more at their fingertips than any previous generation. Many hopelessly seduced by comfort, escape, celebrity, and the vanity of being seen. Browsing had more to do with wandering than exploring. Wanderers left invisible trails, like phantoms. Explorers took great pride in their discoveries, planted flags. Bookmarks. Issues of humanity, crisis of society, took the form of passing phantoms. They lived next to us, right under our noses, but it took tragedy to hold our collective attention, which spanned for a predictable fifteen minutes as long as we were somewhere else living at a safe distance. We loved to watch people of power fall. We liked watching them rise. Loved picking them apart. Outfits. Hairstyles. This, soon, took its effect. Exchanged philosophies less. Gossip and the latest news more. Stared at tragedy from safer regions. Cried into the camera when it was our turn. Documented everything. And this worked in our favor. Police brutality was captured on film, illicit conversations between politicians were captured on tape, undercover lovers were found out, secrets took on new forms. There were secret accounts, new forms of privatizing messages, ways of (at least on the surface) wiping history, spinning stories. Mostly, we were escapists . . .

Andy Warhol was right. George Orwell was right. James Baldwin was right. Steve Jobs was right. What entertainment had become was wrong. But we all watched and followed along, looking at each other like, "I don't know how this happened but it *is* funny." Reshaped our personalities. How we related to others. Demands to not be ignored. Gestures and Pokes. Brought out new sensitivities. New forms of bullying. Mostly, we were thinking of ourselves. We yearned to share our experiences, what we thought was awesome, what we thought sucked. We were searching for similitude.

Have felt the same before. Have concerned myself with the thoughts of others. Have thought of nothing, no one but myself for days on end. Weighed myself against differences. Have attempted to think different. Differently. Correctly . . . Logic and reason. Spiritual discipline. Myth and magic. Music, and other languages. Have experimented with drugs of all kinds and really, it's simple: fuck it.

(a.)

"Look how they treat us,"

—

. . . *whispers the innocent sister. Her life barely missed her. Then Patience approached and he kissed her. Love's like a transistor. Feelings have features. Innocent creatures distort what love teaches. Trade scriptures for preachers, communion for leeches. Earth's mountainous speakers bombard and boom beat us. On guard to defeat us. You hate us. You need us. You are us. You reek us. The Martyrs and Seekers, sow questions and reap us. More grime than grim reapers. Designer diseases resolved to repeat us. You kill us. You eat us. You grow corn to feed us. You crowd us. You beat us. You crave us. You need us. You slaughter and bleed us. You tax us, harass us, pray, and then eat us. You slay us and feed us, from POTUS to penis, the aborted fetus, the corpses, the meat, us. Make sausage of Jesus. The law says to bleed us. We embody greed, lust. The wrong shepherds lead us.*

"Look how they treat us."

The Televisions Descended from Above

A curtain of light
pours from the top
of the screen.

Everything
is illuminated
before it dissolves.

> A thousand whispering voices
> rise from beneath us.
>
> blues, blacks, purples,
>
> sounds of the sea.

> Dark wood
> slowly pushes through frame.

> Ship
> is an
> afterthought.

> Oh, and there's fog.

Now we are on the ship
crowded within it.

Somewhere
beneath the waves

deep in volcanic caves
we hear a crystal voice
calling our names.

> I am but one of them
> huddled amongst the men.
>
> I am a blood red pen.
>
> I am this page.

Rammellzee at the Battle of the Republic

President of Archeological Indifference
Vice-President of Truth
Secretary of Statistics
Minister of Celebrity Injustice
Chief of Staff & Serpent
Blessed Page-Turner of The Great Book
of Misdeeds and Over-Estimations
Bishop of the Great Climate War
Minister of the Deteriorating Sky
Baron of Epic Boredom and Self-Indulgence
ALL GATHERED NOTABLES
I greet you on behalf of The Great Almighty
who was unable to pull himself from
what many are calling the greatest un-scripted reality show of all-time
the very conducting of your lives and attitudes.
We are very proud of the success of our show and network.
Not only have we successfully created
"racists" "bigots" "arrogant country-men"
"patriots" "heart-less capitalists"
but we have also maintained our position as
The Misbegotten, The Pure of Heart
The Heavenly Dove, The Docile Lamb
and The Forgiving Wife.

If Our Great Almighty
could be with us this evening
He would surely want each and every one of you
to know that He graciously accepts your inability to pay your rent
and that He is willing to allow you to do some of His work
so that we might lesson the gaps between the employed and unemployed.

It's not easy to sit back and allow
countless genocides, watch innocence murdered
see trickery and deceit over-ride common-sense and human compassion
and keep one's thumb held, steadily

on the remote control.

There is a Way of Breaking a Heart
So That the Blood Spills Evenly onto the Page

Earth as first video game.
Loves to press the button.
Gets his first taste of power.
"I can beat Daddy at this!"

Triumph over nature.
Even beats the computer.
It's okay to kill the bad guys.

Gun as remote control.

Now the future.

History: Nailed us

to the clock.

Slavery.

Galactic
Ordering
Dynamic

Sold us
what they
could not
give.

Gave us
values
worth
nothing
but
money.

Drill Rap Lifted from Columbus's Journal and Thus Claimed for Our Beloved Pope the Queen

They approached

the boat

in reddish paint.

Naked

they were staring

at our robes and garments

giving thanks.

Down.

Down
from
the sky.

Down
from
the sky

they seem to think

we came.

When the Ocean was the Internet, U were New to Me

They ordered us
online.

Kept inventory
like The Gap.

Kept records
of slaves through
commodity and
shipping insurance

Listed
how many
were on
each ship
arrived in
each state
each country
each continent
each island
for each year.

Kept track of

how many died
how many got sick
how many got pregnant
how many were
thrown overboard.

It's all written down.

People had paid
good money.

Paid to be
protected against
acts of God and nature.

Invented new business
models
when old ones grew
weary
through constant gaze
and inquiry.

Fought against
transparency

until public image
demanded they
support it.

Fought
for corporations
to be treated as people

using legislation
intended to give
slaves the rights
of humans and citizens.

Blessed is he
who tends
to ignore it.

Beneath the Ruins are Older Ruins

I need
a million mouths
to say this
but I only have
this one.

A million bright
ambassadors
of mourning
mothers' Sun.

As if each cloud
were testament
of trials yet to come

and yet
the sky
was clearer
than its memory.

Earth as
my hard drive.

Sky as
my witness.

Search Engine:
find Indian.

All things
traceable.

Language that
self-corrects.
Control/Shift
population.

Press buttons/take lives.

Press keys/pull triggers.
Shake hands/gain confidence.

> Poison
> by touch.
>
> Quarantine
> the infected.
>
> Fire cannon
> introduce
> modern
> warfare.
>
> Lazy drone
> finds comfortable
> island and expands.
>
> Puts his
> money
>
> where my
> mouth is
>
> holds
> my nose.

The quivering hand.

The body slides
across the floor
And opens
its mouth.

The Brightly-Coiled Serpent

I.
I must be
four or five.

Run out the back door
of my father's church
turn the corner and see
a red, white, and blue
snake chasing its tail.

It's either
a memory

of something
that happened

or memory
of a dream.

One of my first
memories not planted
by a story I was told
of something I did.

A story
I remember
and have
never told.

There is another

of being hit
by a car

of fainting

the moment the car
would have hit me.

The car
squeals
to a stop

The driver
helps me up
and asks
if I'm okay.

I look up as
one of the twins
pass on the sidewalk.

We share a look
as I tell the driver
I'm fine.

I may or may not
have asked the twin
to keep this secret.

It was the night
I gained the privilege
of being able to cross
the street by myself

I think
this is
a real
memory.

The memory

of the snake
may be a dream.

If it is,
it is certainly
the first memory
of a dream
that I recall.

II.
Night of my
high school
graduation

Drunk off Cisco
tiptoeing into
my bedroom.

I dive
for the bed
brushing the
light-switch
with my arm.

I had two
light switches:

overhead
and a strobe.

I fall
asleep
mid-air.

Later that night . . .

I roll on my side

feel a foreign weight
pressed against me.

Tickles
my leg.

I shift
my weight

it moves again.

My worst
nightmare.

Snake
in bed
with me.

Grab it
by its neck
squeeze it tight
and bang its head
against the headboard.

Open my eyes to a
flashing series of stills:

Snake's mouth
fanged open.

Brown body
dangling.

Hand

gripping
neck.

It stops
fighting back,

I collapse
exhausted/thankful.

Close
my eyes
and feel
it move
again.

Jump/grab
its neck
and fling it
across the room.

Snake springs
instantly back
onto the bed.

"This fucker
is fast," I think.

I grab its neck
jump out of bed

smash its head
against the wall.

I squeeze it tight
and give one
devasting knock.

Knuckles swipe
the light switch.

Look down and see
my right hand
gripping my left wrist.

III.
Running
through
grass

at the banks
of a river.

Snakes leap
like rabbits
crossing high
in front of me

zoom past
like arrows

I am not scared.

Like running
with horses/wolves . . .

I dream this
while living
in Paris.

IV.
In four years
I will walk to the banks
of the Hudson.

Riverside/158th.

"Wasn't this in
The Warriors?"
I will think
descending
the metal steps.

I will imagine
a small boat
carved from tree
perched beside
the rocks.

One bird will blossom
into a flock—flecks of
turquoise in their wings.

Small man in reddish
paint climbs out of boat

walks through me.

I turn/see
the city
is a forest.

This only
lasts a second

and then
I remember
the dream.

The Funk Is Its Own Reward

The ghosts of all
the young black boys
killed in Chicago for the
year, appear foot-
working on the White
House lawn at dawn.

Rep yo
clique

Rep yo
clique

Rep yo
clique

ripping through
the wires.

It begins
like this.

A little
behind
the beat.

The buzz
of the sirens.

The hazy
monitors of
East Wing
surveillance.

The phone ring.

The knock
on the door.

Where your
ghost at?

Where your
ghost at?

The children
start to rise.

Is us us?

Is is us?

It comes in
like this.

Is us us?

Is is us?

A little
behind
the beat

Broad daylight
French Quarter
Bottle-cap tapping
in Jordans.

. . .

Now if black ghosts
dance, do the native
ghosts read wind?

Is it fair to say
general stereotypes
follow beyond death?

That moment
you realize
your imagination's
been colonized
by self-same
bullshit that made
oblivious maidens
ghost-twerk
in Victorian corsets.

Historic Landmarks

I.
Twenty-eight rooms
nine fireplaces
six bathrooms

double corridors
"so servants
do not interfere
with family life."

The porch has
large white columns.

The house is built
by Stanford White.

No ghosts here
only a constellation
of light pins and
shadows that scroll
walls like reels/film
in a projector's booth.

First
at the top
of the stairs.

Dark
wooden door
slides in and out
of frame.

Fireplace
of jade-green
marble.

The circular walls
painted electric blue.

Perfect for
my nightly game
of shadow-morphing.

Bedtime

wide awake.

The shadows begin
their nightly ritual:

The parade
of chariots
morph into
a herd of buffalo
and circle
'round me.

II.
Memory
the process
in which information
is encoded, stored,
and retrieved.

Stanford White's story
woven into mine.

His death, the birth
of the American tabloid.

His murderer

America's first
"playboy."

His mistress,
America's first
supermodel.

His father
America's foremost
Shakespearean
scholar of the time.

The morphing images

the hidden rooms

and beneath them

the trial
of my century.

Daylight comes
and I have no memory
of falling asleep.

III.
Dear God
We come today
on the verge
of yesterday

so close, yet
so far away

miles from
the center.

Oh God,
on bended knee
you stand just
as tall as me.

Set it right
or set me free.

Teach me
good dementia.

IV.
My mother teaches
Sunday school
heads the youth
fellowship
and teaches
kindergarten at
my elementary school

Horizons on
the Hudson.

A magnet between
a cemetery and
the projects.

The cemetery
has a bike path

a popular
short cut

to Liberty Street.

The local mortician
my father's best friend

is the richest
black man in the city.

He lives in another
historic landmark
just blocks away
and tips me nicely
for delivering
his paper.

I wake at four,
fold the papers,
and ride my bike
through the cemetery.

I pass the school,
churches, liquor stores
and abandoned houses.

I have
never heard
of "white flight"
yet somehow grasp
that this poverty is in
direct relation to
the hidden rooms
morphing images
of the projector's booth
where shadows bleed
from light and betray
their powered
source of governance.

There are screens
beyond the booth
that portray

a clearer picture
of our misery
simply by showing it
to none.

I learn of the secret
intelligence's role in
supplying drugs
long before they
admit to it.

I wage a
healthy distrust.

I am not allowed
to play with guns.

My parents fear
police will shoot
before realizing
it's a toy.

My mother tells me
that if I am stopped,
to place both hands
on top of the steering
wheel and tell
the officer

"I am reaching
for my wallet."

I must be
four or five.

She says
if I'm drafted

into the Army
we'll move
to Canada.

One day
I return from school
and tell my parents
I want to be an actor.

My father says
"I'll support you
as an actor
if you get
a law degree."

My mother suggests
I do my next
school report
on Paul Robeson.

That night in the
projector's booth
figures run
through forests

a crowd
applauds wildly
trees fan
the shadows.

I tilt my head
and see a world.

V.

Dreams are successions
of images, ideas, emotions,
and sensations that occur
involuntarily in the mind
during certain stages
of sleep.

I am wide awake.

Paid Advertisement 1

<== Father begins

I asked her
to clean up
her room.

She said,
"I'm not a slave."

"Nuh, duh," I said,
"cause if you were,
with that attitude,
you'd be dead."

"No. I would be
like Harriet Tubman
or Sojourner Truth.
And in honor of
Black History Month,
I won't clean up my room!"

"In honor of the maids
who worked long hours
for little or no pay, who
cleaned and cleaned,
and cleaned, and cleaned . . .
I won't clean up today!"

"Well, you sure do know your history,"
I said. "Girl, you make me proud.

And in honor of your mixed ancestry,
You should clean the house!"

The Answer to the Question that Wings Ask

Is it a quest
or celebrity?

Validation?

A desire to be seen
as one who counts?

To be among
the counted?

A limited number
of seats given to some
denied to others.

The latest American
religion, taking off where
Scientology
left off?

The Great
Mind Control.

The belief
you can become.

The belief
that you can know?

Is it a matter
of cultivating envy?

Making others wish
they could have
what you have,

live the life you live?

The God of those who
beat the odds.

Cultivating talent?

Investing
10,000 hours?

Cultivating ideas
or exploiting them?

Thinking of what others
have not thought of?

Making communication
easier.

Exploiting the unknown?

Fulfilling people's
unwanted desires?

Making them feel
they can't live without
something they have
always lived without?

Is it self-actualization
or self-image
actualization?

Is it the desire
to see one's name in

print
or in lights?

Do the successful
escape the everyday
travails
of worry,
disappointment,
debt, and doubt?

Heroes?

Mothers?

Martyrs?

Is it about self-sacrifice
or having to sacrifice
nothing?

Is it about changing
the times in which we
live?

Exercising compassion
through entrepreneurial
individualism?

Striking gold?
Being of service?

The Golden Rule?

Divine intentions?

Raising families that
share those intentions?

Is it more about
ambitions than
intentions?

Setting a goal?

Having a drive?

Libido?

Are we acting out
a sexual fantasy?

To control?

To dominate?

To be controlled?

To be dominated?

Is it about
philosophy?

Described and
prescribed
patterns of thought?

Delineating
a structure,
a framework?

Are we talking
to ourselves?

Are we addicted?

Cultivating addiction?

Should we replace
weed with tobacco,
or tobacco with weed?

Water with wine,
wine with water?

Sugar with
honey or agave?

Meat with tofu?

Ridding ourselves of
toxins, is that it?

Ridding ourselves
of the unwanted,
the undesireable,
the unhealthy?

Are your thoughts
simply an echo
of how you feel?

Are your feelings
as good as thoughts?

Can you distinguish
between the two?

What is the purpose?

Money?

Does that solve
the problem?

What is
the problem?
What is the question?

Will how I ask
the question,
determine
the answer?

What time is it?

Who set
the clock?

Who coded/
decoded time?

Are there
different ways
of keeping it?

What is
the standard?

What is the
guiding principle?

Get rid of fear?

Every individual
knows what it feels like.

Everyone is wrapped
in their own emotions,

beliefs, timelines, and
connections.

You can make
as much sense of it
as you wish, or retreat
into your shell
of beliefs and disbeliefs.

Will you observe,
take action, build
contribute, sit back,
doubt, grow fat
through comfort or
through worry?

What if nothing
you are convinced of
is actually the case?

What if it works
the way it does
in your presence
because it's what
you expect of it?

What if the truth
is not enough?

What if it is not
enough to be sincere
in your actions and
deeds?

If you must also
learn to listen
and not to blame?

To see your own faults
and not list those
of others?

What if
the other
is a lie?

If nothing is original,
Unique, or without
purpose?

What if it means
that you must
sometimes
sit in silence and not
defend yourself?

What if you are
not alone
and alone,

unable to see
the reason or
understand,
and your understanding
in all its glory
manages to still
get in the way?

What if your mind
works against you?

What if it is simply
not your time

and the stars

are right where
they belong for it all
to make sense?

And if you choose
not to believe it?

What if you are
too tired to write
or think and the music

is too loud to
concentrate
or fall asleep?
what if when you
turn off the music,
your mind starts
to orchestrate the
silence

and every creak of wood

the wind through trees

the call of birds

Your heartbeat

is enough
to dance?

Dance.

Unanimous Goldmine

All Coltrane solos at once!

Twist them horns
'round the necks
of each equation
and expand upon
multiples of death.

We were crowded
into the shitbins
of a floating toilet
dreaming of
an afterlife.

Memory stored
in a cloud.

Terrabytes
sea-major.

Winners of
religious thinking
praise books
for bookends.

Here is
the invention
of the astronaut.

First Nation
Sweat ceremony
In a spaceship.

To imagine hell
is privilege.

Paint a dreamworld
solid enough
to hold us.

Held by blocks of time
margins and calendars
divisions of labor
contracts: social
and otherwise.

With each kiss
bio-dynamic in
direct co-relation
to stars and seasons
the ability to calculate
distance, harness power
stem cells erect mobile mansions
capable of projecting destruction
at greater and greater will, what could
be holding us here?

Here is what
death is like:

Life without fear.

I, for One, Am Happy They Keep Casting
White Actors to Star in Old Testament Flicks

You're supposed to
thank God for giving
it to you before you
actually have it.

That way God
peeps your faith
and is like,
*Yo, you saw it
in yourself
Never doubted
I would deliver*
and BOOM, voila.

Luckily, God
updated himself.

That Old Testament
shit was getting tired.

Demanded
they murder
the first-born

was on some
genocide shit.

But God
straightened up,
had a name change.

Got himself born
in Brooklyn.

Sang regularly on a
television show
as a kid.

Got paid
nine dollars
a minute.

Stretch notes
for money.

School of
the Arts.

Sat beside
Lando Calrissian
in math class
before becoming
a cop.

The LAPD imported
cops from southern
states as their black
ghettoes started getting
out of hand.

That's the problem
with these kinds of
poems.

Put a cap in 'em
watch words ≠ topics
start buckin 'round.

Boycotted Coca-Cola
for being bout that
bizness regardless
the bullshit the mthrfckrs
who drank it practiced.

Their argument
"Well, water, don't
discriminate."

"It made sense
for the times."

It was an agreed
upon reality.

What we knew
and practiced.

And so the story goes . . .

I stood outside
and smoked a spliff
before writing this.

Call it "a ritual."

The curve
of the street
keeps me
hidden.

Can spot

police before
they spot me.

Hand in ready position
for disposal.

Neighborhood
heavily patrolled.

The existence
of simple truths
still a crime.

There's always
the chance
a NGH like u
might star
in something
other than
a police report.

But police—like
the Old Testament gang—
mostly just follow orders.

Alternative Reality, in Which We Learned to Disappear

Heaven as
a police state.

Others imagine
a free market.

Heaven on earth.

God bestowed religion
upon humanity. Suffering
as a discipline and with that,

we learned to disappear.

Before we were hunted,

before they came
to steal us,

before we were sold,

before we were pushed away,

quarantined, stripped of inalienable rights,

before
a rape

as literal as transparent

(doesn't hide its motives),

we learned to disappear.

And with us, the bees.

Now they scared.

Warded Like Music, by Measures

The patrons of jazz
funded funerals
in funhouses.

African Fractals
for future reference.

Congo squared
divided by train tracks.

Warded
like music
by measures.

Sustained my breath
and held down
my whole note.

Bubbles cascade
over parallel lines,
etched in stretch
down her thighs.

Held my head
against pull
of undertow.

The bathtub ring
circled my eyes.

Drained
of everything
that had once tried
to drown me.

Decades of
environmental
degradation.

Mismanagement
of the levee system.

Poverty overcame
patience.

History
headed
by hounds.

The pacing
of the dirge.

The crumbling
of my infrastructure.

I caved in.

I felt neglected.

You had
abandoned me.

She seemed what
I was missing.

Filled my glass
as soon as
I emptied it.

Lent her voice
to sing my song.

Her kiss shook me
more than I expected.

Took me straight
where I belong.

The firming
of the foundation.

The hardening
of fresh concrete.

The diasporic
shift of center.

Washed away
my sins.

Washed
my feet.

How much
are we subject
to the history
we reference?

If we sing
of mighty battles,
will we conjure them?

The siege of Orleans

Joan of Arc,
in her 12th year,
saw God.
Black boys
dancing on
bottle caps
heard voices.

Strangled
in dance step.

Sourced from
the broken wind
of overgrown seas.
Hormones

within the wave.
Dismantled
more black keys
than white.

Some songs
we cannot sing.

The Disappearance of the O

Clarity
that renders
us blind.

Nothing
to see
here.

Humanity
condones
persecution,
oppression
of its saints.

Nothing
t see.

The rigin f w w.

The perfection end wed in the give and take f breath and air, the pumping heart
and generat r, the electrifying f rce f magnetism, mysticism, the unseen hidden
chart and path thr ugh bl d and vessel, sea within seas, and sees all that is bef
re it, the wind thr ugh trees, the rush f waves, herds f animals, c l rs and smells,
f birds, f rests, villages and cities, c l rs f paint and hair, eyes, the shapes f m
uths and   n ses, n ises and s unds, s ngs, yes, f music.

Everything n the page
but n thing f r the ear t see.

Dead beat

dead beat
begat break
beat

    break
beat begat
dope beat

dope beat
begat trap
beat

    trap
beat be dat

gat beat

gat gat

make a
NGH NGH
NGH do

gat gat

make a
NGH NGH
NGH do

gat gat

make a
NGH NGH
NGH do

do that
do that
do that
gat gat

Fck the Beliefs

Some thoughts travel
from distant places

are not born
within our borders

must pass through
heightened security

fortified by
age old tradition

norms of societal culture

misgivings of prejudice
and misplaced judgment

in order
to arrive
peacefully
in our minds.

Our minds
high-walled fortresses
where security councils
gather to preserve
comfort
enforce
what we have
been taught to value
discern and determine
what is real.

We depend
on our minds

to guide and aid us
from one day
to the next.

Some of us see our
minds like muscles
we exercise

with theorems, riddles,
thought and thought
processes.

We gather
and store
information.

Play word games
rap, solve problems
work to the best
of our abilities.

We accept/reject labels
and categorizations at
face value.

We sometimes choose
lifestyles based upon the
accepted
labels we identify with,
which then take the form
of "beliefs."

Beliefs are
the police
of the mind.

They are either
uniform or universal
armed or unarmed.

They hold the power
to confiscate material
they consider hazardous
or incredible.

They profile experience
and information as:
"Bullshit." "Nonsense."
"Get the fuck
out of here."

They convene regularly
with the thought security
council and act
according to their
constitution of what is
real or unreal,
possible or impossible,
and they are sometimes
and often mistaken.

MY question is:

What is your mind's
immigration policy?

Do you detain
foreign thoughts
that may have entered
your mind illegally

against the wishes
of your parents
pastors, teachers

or simply against
the security
of your own comfort?

Are there other thoughts
you have allowed to go
unchecked,
unquestioned,
because they seem
aligned
with your so-called
"identity"?

Are you certain
you are not a victim
of identity fraud?

Glorybox

Fck G-d
where u
find her and call it
a day.

The tragedy
that begat
the Sun
made light
of lesser things.

It was an explosion.

First in heart.   Now at hand.

This tree's blood
is painted on.

The guilt
that I feel

is freedom.

Jesus was
the only magic
we believed in.

The cigarette
that tricked us
into breathing.

An excuse to sing.

Anthemic woodwind
hollow as crown
fall through the octaves
glide over ground and come to me.
Crosses as crutches.
Christ on crooked feet.

King of the Shoes.
Carcasses crafted by hand.

Some are the lives we walk on.

Coltan as Cotton

Hack into
dietary sustenance —
tradition vs. health.

Hack into
comfort/compliance.

Hack into the
rebellious gene.

Hack into doctrine.

Capitalism
in relation
to free labor
and slavery.

Hack into
the history of bank.

Is beating the odds
a mere act of joining
the winning team?

Hack into
desperation
and loneliness.

The history of
community
and the marketplace.

Hack into land rights
and ownership.

Hack into business law
proprietorship.

Hack into ambition
and greed.

Hack into forms
of government.
The history of
revolutions

Their relation to suffering
and sufferance.

Hack into
faith and morality

the treatment of one
faith towards another.

Hack into masculinity
femininity/sexuality

what is taught
what is felt
what is learned
what is shared?

Hack into God

stories of creation
serpents and eggs.

Hack into nature

bio-dynamics
bio-diversity
cycles and seasons.

Hack into time

calendars
Descartes
its relationship to doubt
is it wired to fear
the notion of control
the space/time
continuum

the force of gravity
whether
the opposite
of gravity
is freedom?

Hack into freedom
power
responsibility
justice
the Bill of Rights.

Hack into coincidence

the summer of '68
the 27 Club
the number of people
with Facebook profiles

people who

choose to share
people who
share too much
people who
seem lonely
people who
want to connect
people who
want to uplift
people who
need uplifting.

Hack into self-help
self-sufficiency and
self indulgence.

Hack into crazy.

Hack into lunatic.

Hack into star.
Hack into
infamous/notorious.

Hack into narcissism

the effects
of poverty
on the psyche

the effects of race
the effects of cruelty

the victims
that survived.

There is a panel

marked Survival.

*Three simple
copper wires
coiled 'round an orb.*

Hack into orbit

equatorial
land mines

useful and
precious metals

COLTAN AS COTTON.

Hack into hazardous

nuclear blue clear
cloud form and fish farm
cow farts and pig shit.

Hack into horse
industrial—digital.

Hack into code.

Use your instrument
as metaphor.
Harness your craft.

Hack into the mainframe.

Dismantle
definition
dogma
and duty.

Hack into destiny.

Hack into dreams

subtext and
subconscious

Hack into heart

cardio-Congo
blood rich in oil.

Hack into
suffering and despair.

Hack into the unfair
advantage of those
lucky enough to be born
into one family or
another
into one condition or
another.

Hack into the
circumstantial
evidence that proves the
obvious and wakes the
oblivious.

Hack into birthright

bloodlines:

royal and tainted.

Hack into superstition

old wives tales

the rituals of
the shaman.

Hack into chemistry

the pharmaceutical
industry

the modern rape
of the forest.

Hack into DNA

the coiling serpents

the time it takes
for modern man
to determine whether
ancient men were foolish
or not.

Hack into
the database.

Hack into the
subconscious

the panel marked

survival.

Hack into celebrity.

Hack into the cultural
development of taste.

Hack into violence
fear and ignorance.

How are they linked?

Paid Advertisement 2

little girl's voice begins==>

My grandma
had an afro
that was larger
than the Sun.

She wore big shoes
that made her tower
over everyone.

She said
weird things like

"Groovy Baby"

"We Shall Overcome"

and "Power to the People!"

with a black hat
and a gun

But now
she's soft
and cuddly and her hair's
braided and gray.

She took me
to the White House
on Inauguration Day.

And when
our brand new president
walked out onto the stage
she looked at me and said

"My, my, my . . .
How things have changed."

Paid for by Armchair Revolutionaries For Symbolic Change

You Can't Unring the Bell

10,000 hours
in meditation
and the orator appears.

He speaks of what
he sees and feels.

He speaks beyond
his years. I hear
myself in every word
as if he were my mind.
Aligned with all
I thought to say
as if he were my kind.
Species of the spirit
all in blood and all in breath.
Children of a gentler hand
begin again at death.
Softest petal
of the rose
descends
unto the Earth.
Spreads her legs
to part the seas and dies
while giving birth.

What's it worth?

If angels
will not
stop a train
from running
off its tracks

If God
would judge
each passenger
and kill us all
in packs

Let's smoke crack.

Satchmo's Smile Is Contagious

How many voices
did they silence
when through
voice alone,
they heal?

How they sang
through ancient wisdom
what time
would count
to kill?

When conspiracies
of silence
were the loudest
in the room

and the light
of dawn
stood just outside
like life beyond
the tomb?

How many voices
did they wrangle
from the spiraled
neck of sound

when it hung
between shoulders

and the head
was tilted
down?

What became
of all the music
that would
breathe through
steel and glass

that would glide
over the surface
like rides of
souped-up past?

And the sounds
that slowly penetrate
the pinkened flesh
within

like a
clever thought
that touches off
where muscles form
a grin.

And the grin
that crawled
into a smile

to stand
on teeth
again.

How I Got Over

Lift me up
so I can
tell them

how you came
to cut the ropes

that had blossomed
like the strangest fruit

descending
from my hopes.

And when I
thought my neck
would crane

to see
what level eyes
could not

I felt the ground
beneath my feet
and listened.

Subharmonic symphony
swelling from beneath.

Mastery over mystery.

Worlds beyond belief.

Karma of
the buffalo.

Innocence
was lost.

Suffering was
the death
of me.

Freedom
had a cost.

How I got over.

I had betrayed
him with a kiss
is how they told it.

Convinced myself
to trust each soul
encountered.

Believed my honesty
could only reap truth.

Destroyed the fear
which kept me
from my calling.

Absolved myself
from history's
dangling
noose.

Yet still
rivers

to cross,
mountains
to climb.

Weapons
worn by
passing soldiers
sang to me.

Angry women
kissed and licked
their names
into me.

Forty days
if decades
were knights.

Whole cavalries
fought youth.

Time is a
privatized prison.

Beauty manipulated.

Timeless standard
of give and take

and all
that love
would give.

Forgiven

for freedom.   time.   To be love.

To be abandoned by   To be loved.

Manhattan Beach

I rose to find
the setting Sun
a stone
beneath
my feet.

And as I stepped
beyond that stone
and it stayed
in its place

I felt a new warmth
taking shape
from deep and hidden
space.

I do not
breathe
the same.

My chest
is a cathedral.

My ribcage
frames stain glass

The story on each panel
says
new Suns are rising fast.

And my means
have more precision.

And my needs

are fueled by waste.

And I'm channeling
an alchemy
that smells

just like it tastes.

And the depths
that I am reaching
are the heights
that I foresee.

And the people
give to nature
what was taken
from the sea.

And the children
slowly gathered.

None of them
had ever seen.

None of them
had dared imagine

how their lives
looked from a dream.

There's no other
way around this.

It's internal,

buried deep.

Beneath labyrinthine
thought tunnels
where the questions
pile in heaps.

Heaped upon that
is a mystery.

Heaped upon that
is a plan.

Heaped upon that
the simplicity
of a river
through
the land.

And the cows
around that river
do not graze
unto the sea.

They are inland
bred and treasured
through their
own complicity.

And the answers
are apparent.

Difference
is all the same.

I'm a whale of deepest
regions
where the ocean floor's
aflame.

And the source
of this great fire
is internal

buried deep

where the blood
of stars configure
in volcanic memory.

And they push
beyond the surface.

And they push
upward and out.

From the source
of our great sorrows
to the pucker of a
mouth.

Kiss.
Kiss.
Kiss.

Another century.

Kiss.
Kiss.
Kiss.

Another year.

Kiss.
Kiss.
Kiss.

Another species.

Kiss.
Kiss.
Kissed

to disappear.

And we kiss
to cross the threshold
to our present
state of mind

where our feelings
fly from memories
that rest behind
the eye.

And our dreams
are deep polluted
by such tragedies
as wealth.

And the fish
forget they're
swimming.

And the fins
morph into tails.

And the truth
like evolution
is evolving
as it fails

to keep up
with the demands
of this modern
space and sea.

And the skyline
of this city

are the whales
we used to be.

And I feel
these kids
around me

as I'm perched
on sandy shore.

And they're
touching me
and asking
if I'd like
some water
or
if I'm
already dead?

So I open
up my eye

and I'm staring
through an arid wind
at white whales in the
sky.

And I notice
how they're
floating.

And I wonder
if they see

distant cousins
in the world
beneath

where skies
are buried
deep.

Orca Before He Swallowed the Black Box

It is a sickness
that begins
in the mind.

An insecurity
that blossoms
into fear.

It is where
compassion ends.

The phallic
that gives.

The phallic
that takes.

A precursor to death
and mortality.

The father who
hates his son
for his youth.

The shadow
that overshadows
its source.

You reek
of the death
you harvest.

You, who warp
genius into factory

propagate poisons.

It has come to this.

Paid Advertisement 3
Black History Month

kid's voice begins==>

Paul Robeson had a deep voice.
Deeper than Darth Vader too!

He toured the globe for freedom
like that Dalai llama dude.

He sang in many languages
and starred in movies too

but used his art to fight for
what was fair and what was true.

One day when I came home from school
I said to Mom and Dad

When I grow up I want to sing! Perform! I want to act!"

Dad said that he'd support me
if I got a law degree.

"Well, Paul Robeson did that, son,"
my mom said, "Go check and see."

So I looked and saw
he practiced law
but only for a week
because some silly secretary
wouldn't write when he would speak!

Instead he chose to sing and speak
and bravely pave the way
for every man who speaks
when history won't write what he says.

*Paid for by the Negronomers Hand Trust

Outlawed Animal Arguments for Vegans

On _____, the United Nations General Assembly condemned the massacre and declared it to be an act of genocide. The voting record on section D of Resolution 37/123 was: yes: 123; no: 0; abstentions: 22; non-voting: 12.

The delegate for Canada stated: "The term genocide cannot, in our view, be applied to this particular inhuman act." The Soviet Union, by contrast, asserted that: "The word for what _____ is doing on _____ soil is genocide. Its purpose is to destroy the _____ as a nation." The delegate of Singapore—voting yes—added: "My delegation regrets the use of the term 'an act of genocide' . . . as the term 'genocide' is used to mean acts committed with intent to destroy, in whole or in part, a national, ethnic, racial or religious group." The Nicaragua delegate asserted: "It is difficult to believe that a people that suffered so much from _____ would use the same fascist, genocidal arguments and methods against other peoples." Canada and Singapore questioned whether the General Assembly was competent to determine whether such an event would constitute genocide.

The United States commented that "While the criminality of the massacre was beyond question, it was a serious and reckless misuse of language to label this tragedy genocide as defined in the 1948 Convention . . .".

Pattern Against User

To be enslaved
to that which we
have been born into
with no founded
route of escape is
what it is.

Allows looming
possibility of surprise.

Fuck around
and turn out
mesmerizing.

How did you
come up with that?

Easy.

Force a million people
onto a spaceship
transport them
to another planet
take away
their liberties
ban their
drums/phones
keep them concentrated
in camps four hundred years
or at least thirteen generations
of rape, murder,
enslavement

add touch of trumpets
and bid them play.

Middle fingers, all day.

Oceanium

And when water
was the enemy

after tears
became the sea

and eyes, like doors, were opened
by a wisdom carved from trees

and the forest
was a playground

where the children
stood in place

logged into
the sunken structures
where the pillars
had a face

and the taste of freedom withered
when it lived inside the walls

so it sprang
into the open

where the bathrooms
had no stalls

and the waves of water cleansed us
and the taste of freedom lived

add a touch
of what we came for

and a pinch
of what it is

and the salt
is in the water

and the water
feeds the trees

and the sun
a single flower

and the mountains
bend their knees
and the waves break into laughter
and the ocean sparks aflame

and the sadness
walks on water

'til it takes another name.

To Drown in Baptism

Darkness and then darkness.

Waves of
despair. Moaning.   A stolen metaphor, slain parable. Death and
details.

A crushing of the spine. A splaying of the
senses.

We were transformed.

Is the caterpillar

informed of its becoming?

Does it enter its cocoon
fearing death, and watch
its painful blossoming
in slow motion,

never sensing

an end?

What if it imagined
its cocoon its deathbed?

Tried to figure out
How things had
led to this?

Imagined
it had done
something wrong?

What if I had

listened to my elders

changed my diet   hadn't upset my parents

had made

a single offering ?

It is a clouding of memory.
A slowing of the senses.
A distortion of sound.
A gathering of dust.

Fuck. Fuck. Fuck. What is happening?

A standstill. Too harsh of a reality
to comprehend, The weight of iron

chains.

The rot of flesh.

To drown in baptism.

The extinguishing of the soul.

To barter dreams for life
and then to live
not as you dreamt you would,

yet still to live.

An act of giving thanks.

a way
of seeing   hoping   believing

a matter of

perception,

a matter of time

space
beyond   a sense of maturity   a bit of courage
matter   a sense of exploration   an understanding

                                                                       a vivid comprehension

There is a layer of belief

                                                                       a gut feeling, so much
that holds up to all questioning

                                                                       more than sensation

                    I never doubt this
                    I feel it deeply
                    and sense
                    I can know it.
                                        Embedded
                                    within it is the belief
                                    that we *can* know

                                that things are possible
                                through feeling

                                    through listening

                                    through sensing.

                        The relationship we develop
                        with our intuition

                                            will in many ways
                                                    define us.

                            Do we doubt it?
                            Do we doubt ourselves
                                            Can we trust them?
                            our gut instincts?

Can we trust?

It is not
that there is
no research
no thought
no reasoning
involved

It is simply
a knowing
that there is
something
beyond it

a cloud

of mystery
                lifted

a sense that which
binds and blinds us

a fixed way
of seeing things

of believing

of trusting

more than what
others have said
or handed down
than what you feel

a clinging
to tradition

a refusal to
throw away
our crutches

an overcoming of fear

a breakthrough

a willingness
to exceed the norm,

a determination

a discipline

a dance   a way of placing

in many ways
a way of moving
forward

one foot
in front

backward and around

of another

a means
of coming   spiraling
                                       further out
                                       from the center,

full circle

deeper in

It is not
a mystery   it is a love affair

a willingness
to surrender

a way of rooting
something out

following through

digging deeper

reading stones

overturning dirt

recognizing
 symbols

pulling back
the veil

It is at once:

a kiss   an orgasm

a spasm of release   an epiphany

                                                                    a flick

                                    of a switch that
                                    jolts an electric chair
                                    to shock its detainee
                                    and brings him back
                                    to life. It is not a way
                                    of dying There is no
                                    death in this

                    although
                    centuries
                    of despair   years of solitude
                                      mostly in communal
                                      gatherings where we   A way of praying
                    Yes.   sang, danced, prayed.   of giving thanks

                                                of connecting dots
                                                much more than hope

            an increased
            sense of knowing

                                                            of learning
            a willingness
            to overcome   to become

            an expanded
            sense of being

all we have ever hoped

but could not dream   could not imagine

life after death

after thought

after breath

it is a whisper

a piercing scream
deep in the night

These Mthrfckrs

These mthrfckrs don't want to back down, Aye Aye Aye.
These mthrfckrs don't want to back down, Aye Aye Aye.
These mthrfckrs don't want to back down, Aye Aye Aye.
These mthrfckrs don't want to back down, Aye Aye Aye.
These mthrfckrs don't want to back down, Aye Aye Aye.
These mthrfckrs don't want to back down, Aye Aye Aye.
These mthrfckrs don't want to back down, Aye Aye Aye.
These mthrfckrs don't want to back down, Aye Aye Aye.
These mthrfckrs don't want to back down, Aye Aye Aye.
These mthrfckrs don't want to back down, Aye Aye Aye.

Child of
the diaspora.

I don't know
what tribe I'm from.

But I'm fighting
for freedom.

Don't believe
in tribe no more.

Child of the
messiah's whore.

And I'm fighting for freedom,
justice, and then some.

These mthrfckrs don't want to back down, Aye Aye Aye.
These mthrfckrs don't want to back down, Aye Aye Aye.
These mthrfckrs don't want to back down, Aye Aye Aye.
These mthrfckrs don't want to back down, Aye Aye Aye.
These mthrfckrs don't want to back down, Aye Aye Aye.
These mthrfckrs don't want to back down, Aye Aye Aye.

As If Thighs Were Parentheses

What my fame
affords me
I will use
to spread
the light

that is caused
by the book
that burns
to clean the air
at night.

There are some
that would
save the book
and others
that would write.

There are those
who would die for it
and soldiers
who would fight.

I have learned
of this book
that burns
that it cannot
be helped.

There are words
that will catch aflame
as others tend to melt.

There are phrases
soft turns of speech

that shake flesh
to the bone.

There are ways
of our saying things
that shape truth
into poems.

Or perhaps
they outline a shape
in fact already there

like the face
of my sweet beloved
framed by unruly hair.

And these strands
are just words combined
to comb through
with your eyes.

They are wigs
over mountaintops

the snow
that draws
the eye.

They are there
when you see
them not.

What man
sees his
own heart?

He is drugged
then put to sleep
before he's cut apart.

And procedures
like this only done
when arteries
are clogged.

Spills and waste
down the mountainside
with forests cut
and logged.

All the trees now
shaped into books
and building-blocks
designed will take
shape from the
mountainside
the forest
of the mind.

And the mind
is an active place
where climate
will control
means of growth
and the greenery
that springs up
from the soul.

And the soul
it is like the soil
as i am into u.

What begins
as a seed of thought
now manifests as true.

It takes time
for a rock to melt
to decompose
a corpse.

And the soil
full, rich with time
like mountains
rich with quartz.

Full of charge.
Full of energy.
Full of nutrients
and life
sucked from death
which is overturned
and risen
to new heights.

Over time
life repeats itself

the cycle of the wheel.

And the will
is a driving force
to feed defend and kill.

What it kills
takes a different shape
as consciousness
transforms.

Laws emerge
to defend new life
and thus
new crimes are born.

And what's born
from a spinning wheel
is willed and welled
to shape.

Forms emerge from
the sculptor's hand
nuanced by love
and hate.

And the hate is
grown out of love
of comfort and control

and is shaped
by the overgrowth
of fear/hope
decomposed.

We compose
with creators' hands
the music of the mind.

We choose words
like piano keys
to ease thought
into chime.

And we chime
upon everything
and every sound

we hear.

We diffuse
all times
ticking bombs
to distill hope
from fear

And the hope
that we plant
we tend.

We water
trim and cut.

Like the grape
on its path to wine
we smash
beneath
our strut.

And we strike chords
with expertise.

We lean into
each note.

We give time
a new signature
small hand
on big throat.

All the gun barrels
placed in mouths
all the tongues
fingers   parts

can account
for the silent times
where words
play no part.

Love is art
of the give and take
the build and break
the bends.

It is found
in a simple kiss
the laughing bliss
of friends.

And our friends
are our enemies

are much more
than they seem.

They are tall
booming beams
of light with their own
hopes and dreams.

We form teams
nationalities
taking sides with
our own.

We commit
to our fantasies
our prayers
and our poems.

And these poems
how they turn
to dust

how they
blossom with time
like the seed
that the farmer plants
with bare hands
in the mind.

And my mind
feels the brush of wind
takes strangers in
notes signs.

It is coaxed
by the pretty face
Egyptian lace
the kind.

And it broods
in its silent place
and stirs
when she calls.

And it prays for
a peaceful space
and answers
to Saul.

But it knows
it knows
none of it
and it blurs
by the feed.

It prefers
all the gentler things
and cyclically bleeds.

And it bleeds
flowing streams
of words through
the silence of night.

Softest page
of her inner thigh

she asks
"What would
you write?"

I would
write of a
burning book.

How each thought
stood alone.

How the words
had formed families
sheltered from
the unknown.

How the unknown
would come again
for the words
could not hide

truths and meanings
they held within
when the pen

.

took no sides

And the pen
could be fingertips

softest tongue
against flesh

little toes
against calves
and neck
behind ear
with soft breaths.

And the writing
became the walls
and proposed
new design

until silence
took charge again
and disposed
of the mind.

How she laughed

when I told her that.

How she smiled
and she stirred.

How the room
took a different light.

How the lights
beamed and blurred.

All the lights
of the city gleamed
as if all burned
at once.

All the thoughts
gently laid
to rest

the bequest
of new Suns.

And the books
that would hold
these thoughts

were the Suns
that now burned
in small rooms
that were just like this
where we basked
and took turns.

And the spotlights
that shine on me
navigate every touch.

I am moved
to the darkest space
where small stanzas
erupt.

And eruptions
they blind and quake
when too close
to the site.

As if thighs
were parentheses
holding silence
in light.

Freedom Virus Found in Monkeys

I have never fucked
a louder bitch
than Freedom
on her cycle.

That moment
when you touch
her neck

her eyes say
"Yes, please strangle."

She leans into
your tightening grip
while fighting
for
an angle
and when
she regains
consciousness
she mounts
orangutangal.*

*Now baby,
if ur reading this
we are weaving through
the painted deserts of Arizona.

A moment ago
I took a picture beside
a mountain of orange rocks
and now a herd of dark brown cows
salute you with old eyes.

The mountains are as beautiful
as you remember them
same dream same van
same unfolding path
leading me always
to you.

(b.)

GLORYBOX
An American Dream

Deep down,

on the ocean floor a diver came upon a door at the base of a mountainside that stretched into the blue. He knocked three times and waited. Slightly scared, he hesitated before pushing on the door and swimming through. The door shut right behind him as the brightest light did blind him. He closed his eyes then squinted, just enough, so he could see. To his surprise, before his eyes a city that was made of lies was glowing in the distance on a hill that couldn't be.

Could it be? Who'd believe it? Is that all a vision needs? Just the sustenance of breath and the hopes of one who bleeds? Is it how we hold our visions, how we tilt them in the light, that allows their possibility to be more than could or might? And what if "might" were possibility, not just strength and muscle heap? Must we muscle possibility to be all that it can be? Make conditions. Fuck conditionals. Manifest your every dream. But then what becomes of ego?

Up above,

the downward beam.

I long
for Atlantis.

I have no fear.

I have dream work to do.

The art of manifesting.

I've got to stop
bringing home cats.

Stray wanderers
should wander.

Let my heart
be my home.

I live
in my heart.

I lived
in my head.

I dangled
my feet.

I went
back to bed.

I rose
like the Sun.

I worshipped
the Moon.

I denounced the War.

I smoked
weed at noon.

I thought about love
way more than I could.

I gave back to God
some ink writ on wood.

I sat and became
what brings me to stand.

I made a new friend.

I shook a new hand.

I stared in the eye
deep down to the core.

I stepped through the hole
and approached the door.

I opened the door
and entered the soul.

I took her to bed.

I drank from her bowl.

I gave her my love.

I told a few lies
mainly to myself.

I tried and I tried.

I slowly became
the person I was.

I rose to new heights
beyond and above.

And I am happy to be here.

Still, I long for Atlantis.

Black.

1687. Night.
Darkness yields to blue-black. Small splashes of white pop up like distant stars. The darkness takes motion. A brewing storm in the ocean at night. The full moon peeks from a storm cloud. The tip of a large ship slowly sails into frame, like a wooden barge pulling an island. It moves slowly, until its broad side. A white cross is painted on the side of the ship. Under the cross, the word GLORYBOX is painted in red. It begins to rain. The waves crash. A piercing scream through the night.

Interior. Ship.
Darkness. The sound of the scream is loud, as if we're inside a mouth. The scream putters into a whimper. The whimper takes on rhythmic and melodic form. The waves crash from the outside . . .

Black skin in darkest crawlspace. Metal upon skin. Vomit. Its cargo, Africans, chained by ankle and wrist, are being shuffled about by their armed captors in an attempt to keep the ship from capsizing.

We follow eight men chained together as they're being hustled out of the cramped crawlspace to the deck. Two are dead. Another two seem sick. The gunmen holler, push, and shove as if they are herding pigs or horses. The living drag the dead.

Close-up on one man's scarred face. He lays cramped in darkness, muttering through stench and sickness, as loud as his failing voice can.

> **SCARRED MAN**
> Moteko Kolongo
> Moteko Kolengo
> Moteko Kolengo

His eyes stare blankly before his head falls back, lifeless.

Suddenly, there is commotion as more shackled men are being brought on deck.
Women, and children, chained together, are also hustled onto the deck as they are pushed and tormented by the captors.

Slowly, we focus in on one of the women just as one of her wild-eyed captors notices her. She is being tugged by those she is shackled to, standing in the rain as waves crash against the ship. She holds her stomach and looks to the sky.

We see the moon overhead, then we are back on her face as she looks up—straight into the camera————and screams at the top of her voice:

WOMAN
Ama Nyaninga
Ama Nyaninga
Ama Nyaninga

Cut To:

Present, Brooklyn.
A blue-black painting of a pair of eyes looking up—
Slowly, we see paintings piled against the wall—all revealing close-ups of the horrors of the ship—some too close to distinguish yet made beautiful by texture and color of the paint.

-a hand holding a ship
-a brown ship in blue-black night
-brown body parts woven together

Aria walks into frame—denim, lived in T-shirt—turns on the stereo, writes in red paint over the open mouth, "A-a Nyan-ga, A-a Nyan-ga, A-a Nyan-ga."

We notice an open window and a fire escape beyond where she paints.

Cut to:

Roof of same building: a six-story city dwelling surrounded by others. What we see on the roof is vaguely reminiscent of the sea captain's roof in *Mary Poppins*- with found objects, street signs, car doors, odd parts all forming the framework of a ship. More picturesque than a junkyard, it is an artistically assembled boat that gives the impression of somebody's clubhouse.

Ah, affectionately known as "Ah Yeah" has been sitting in his clubhouse writing in his journal.

Letters to a sleeping girlfriend.

The past is within us and plagues our perception of the present. At present, I am home, sitting in a ship of my own building, on my building, and I am building a sense of rapport with this new journal. This is my first journal entry. I am writing for my sanity. I am writing to make sense of last night's dream. I am writing because it is the second best—building is the best—business that I can give to my hands when Aria is asleep and I do not wish to disturb her. The Sun is rising and I'm perched on the skyline. Can you see me here, Aria? Here is another letter to be delivered to your sleep.

My presence
sparks the dream. <== pretentious

Are you dreaming, Love?
Without you, would I
have found the patience
to sit here and write?

The workings of a muse.

The simple workings of love.
The dubious workings of sleep.

And if not only must we rest our
bodies but also the space
for barricades we place around
our mind to dissolve.

A story taking place
that we must allow
to tell itself.

Is it a simple collage
of observational experience?

Add humor and you have
the job of a comedian.

The job of the dreamer?

The painter who spreads memory
across the sky and never leaves room
for the Sun.

Born of a Fiery Womb

As if I had the answer
to the questions that u ask.

As if I chose a single time
to sever now from past.

As if the truth
were in my hands.

As if I kept them clean.

As if I chose a single path
and fastened to the dream.

As if the wind
As if the stars
As if the in between
had watched me
in my sleep and
protected me.

As if there were
a single day
so unaligned with stars
that frightened/fearless lovers
might ignite the civil wars
that gave birth to us.

Momentarily distracted by a ladybug crawling on the wall beside him, he hears the music while watching the ladybug. "Aria's up," would be the name of the smile that appears on his face. He closes his journal and heads indoors.

Ah finds Aria lost in thought before a blank canvas coated in red. She doesn't look his way.

Cut To:

City College, Day, Informal Classroom.
Ah stands in front of a class of forty-five students of different shades and backgrounds, all with a common sense of respectful awe for their "professor."

AH:
But what is the difference between hip-hop and poetry? Is there a difference? When there is a distinction to be made it is most likely due to this "competition."

The students _____ - Ah's_____
more friend then professor-_____.

AH:
Emceeing is a competitive art form. No one wants to listen to a rapper unless they claim to be "the best rapper alive." The competitive stance that the rapper takes forces

108

him/her to embody that old hip-hop saying, "act like you know." It is a matter of projecting confidence. The poet, on the other hand, acknowledges that she is still learning—that she is a student trying to figure it out—it is not that she is less confident—rather she is confident enough to openly acknowledge the power of vulnerability.

Aura Purple, a student, raises her hand and speaks.

AURA:
Aren't there exceptions to that rule?

AH:
Well, that's why we're here, Ms. Purple. For you to become the exceptions to these rules. These rules are not set in stone. They are the simple by-products of society, products of observation. And what is more important than the distinction between hip-hop and poetry is what they have in

common, which is through the command of language they tend to effect the experience of the writer and possibly of the person who reads or sings along. They're forms of invocation. Tupac said, "I never had a [criminal] record until I said that I did on record." John Keats said, "Poets are midwives of reality."

All right, that's time for today. Your homework is to finish your "Howl"/ "Planet Rock" comparision—and to record tonight's dream—which I expect to find posted no later than noon tomorrow. And don't forget! Your whole diet! Everything you eat. Everything you read, listen to or watch.

Evening.
A few friends gathered around a driftwood table laden with candles and a few bottles of wine. Tamara, Joan (Ah's mom), and Aria are in the kitchen lighting candles on a birthday cake. They walk into the room with others, singing, "Happy BIrthday to You." Mouths move, people sing, but in Ah's mind there is silence and the image of Aria's face lit by the candles.

Undressed

Kisses
through
thinest
white
veils.

Soft as
the flesh
of breast
that fine-tuned
patience reveals.

She is daylight
in heels.

The humble priest
kneels
to kiss
the cross

of copper
and brass
of symbols
embossed
in flesh.

Religion
is women
undressed.

Tu lips

. . . and if u chose
to memorize
a pair of lips
each day

carried them
to a moment
of silence
and recollection

traced and
retraced them
with pencil
and tongue
lips of a stranger
pressed into
book of flesh
and memory

two stanza
crimsom'd poem
carved into face
where breath
and meaning
might escape.

If u chose
to know
two lips
by heart
by lesser things
like touch
in.dent.ation
with teeth
beneath

softest lips
with tongue

would those
parted seas
swallow
this war?

Interior. Aria's workspace.
Joan looking at Aria's paintings stacked against the wall.

JOAN:

Aria, Honey?
Are these abstract? I feel
like I can vaguely make
out the images, like this
looks like a mouth, a
child in a womb . . . Why
so much repetition? Is it
part of a series?

ARIA:

Well, it's really just what
I remember. It's . . . it's a
recurring dream.

JOAN:

The same dream, Aria?
Not the same dream.

ARIA:

I'm not gonna run this
time, Ms. Bowery. Ah
and I talked about it.
He's having his dream
too. They both started
up again about a month
after I got back. We're
just gonna sit through it
and see where it takes
us. I'm not gonna run.

AH:

(coming to save Aria):
It's alright, Ma. We're
gonna figure it out this

time . . . or just follow it
to its end.

JOAN:
That's what I'm afraid
of. I lost your father to
his dreams.

AH:
We lost Dad to drugs.
It's not the same thing.
Mom, the only thing
we do is get into bed
together and the rest
is . . .

JOAN:
(to Aria)
But baby, last time you
scared us all so . . .

ARIA:
That was years ago, Ms.
Bowery, I'm a woman
now. And, honestly, I
began to miss where my
dreams were taking me.

JOAN:
You can't mean that, girl.

ARIA:
Yes, of course it
wasn't therapy that
helped me. They can't
diagnose an occurrence
that's beyond their
belief. I don't want
the happenings of my

mind drugged out of me so that I fit some silly standard of sanity. I dream what I dream for a reason. The words Ah's able to pull from my paintings take their effect for a reason.

AH:
(attempting to lighten the mood):
And that reason is reason enough for us to be together and figure this shit out. And if the angels conspire to bring my angel back to me for my birthday, sheeeeeeet, Imma let them flap they wings.

Sound of the door opening in the other room.

OKRI:
Where's the birthday boy?

EVERYONE:
Okri!

Horn of the Clock Bike

Red stain
on the co
concrete.

Disdain
for the
bare feet.

Work
Work
my kitango

No perk

for the

bongo.

Who presence is charity?
Who
Who
Who
fresh
from
disparity?

Who
Who
arms
wide
open?
Who
Who
Who

strange
fruit
smokin'?

Paint on a canvas

carved
from a pancreas.

Blue for the water.

Red for the daughter.

Money green

where the land

was.

First
hand

second

second-hand laws.

Thorn
of the
crown-spike.

Horn

of the

clock-bike.

Smile
of the
victor.

Child
of the
prisoner.

Sculptures

of martyrs.

Hackers
as artists.

Shout out
to Atlantis.

First
hand

second

second-hand

us.

Haitian Fight Song

Toussaint
L'Ouverture   in a Gucci fur.

You say
"Look at him."

Bitch, look at her.

Her
by any means

means nécessaire.

Hanging from

a beam

feet

in the air.

. . . at the end of lovemaking. Ah kisses Aria and starts to get up.

                                        ARIA:
                                        (eyes closed)
                                        No, don't sleep out
                                        there. Stay with me
                                        tonight.

                                        AH:
                                        Are you sure? You
                                        should get some rest.

                                        ARIA:
                                        Sleep with me tonight.
                                        I'll be fine, I promise.

                                        AH:
                                        Okay.

Ah cuddles up beside Aria and closes his eyes. A lone bedside candle
allows us to see Aria's closed eyes. Slowly, we begin to see movement
behind the lids.

Darkness, blue-black night, ocean, and a ship that pulls into frame. It is
the same scene as the first, only now we experience everything from the
perspective of the woman who holds her stomach. The rock of the ship is
steady, nauseating, the glow of the moon, the horror of her surroundings,
those enchained, the bestiality of her captors, all in the rhythmic sway of
the sea. She holds her stomach, looks around and notices those in chains
around her begin to drop as if dead. Each one seems to look up and say
something as if for the moon to hear, before they drop. Bodies around her
drop in slow motion. The rhythmic sway of the ship.

                                        AH:
                                        (V.O.)
                                        Three is the beginning
                                        of all things try

angles when wrecks
tangle your wings, let
vision blur not your
deserving see self
as the ghost of your
servings . . .

We pull back and see the white cross painted on the ship. We watch in
slow motion as dead bodies are wrangled from the living and piled on
deck. We reenter the vista of the woman as she observes.

AH:
(V.O.) con't:
If you're serving the
father, there's no Sun
without mother, parent-
bodies discover water-
bodies and drown. Wade
me in the water 'til
Atlantis is found.

We pull back on the face of the woman who with shock and fear in her
eyes makes one last startled look up into the first camera before saying

WOMAN:
Ama Nyaninga.

She falls.

Aria wakes up crying.

AH:
It's okay, love. It's okay.

ARIA:
Ama Nyaninga.

AH:
Ama Nyaninga?

ARIA:
She died. Everybody
was dying. They would
look up at the moon,
say something and then
drop. Ama Nyaninga.
Ama Nyaninga. Ama
Nyaninga.
She was looking right
at me.

AH:
Do you think that's her
name?

Aria nods yes.

AH:
She says her name
three times before she
dies.

ARIA:
They all say it.

AH:
Her name?

ARIA:
No they all say their own
names three times
before they die.

AH:
(under breath)
Beetlejuice. Beetlejuice.
Beetlejuice.

Night.
Ah sits on the couch. He pulls up his laptop. We follow a montage of keywords and images: Atlantis. Legend. Plato. Poseidon. Atlantic. Medusa. Northwest coast of Africa. Volcanoes submerged underwater. Ah types "Transatlantic Slave Trade." "Middle Passage."
"Overcrowded." "Disease." "Death." "Thrown overboard." "Ships followed by sharks." . . .

Morning.
Aria and Ah sipping tea in front of Aria's paintings.

ARIA:
You think I'm crazy?

The Haunt

I always seem
to fall in love
with haunted
women.

The kind
between
thin sheets
of ice and
thread.

A lone one
lurking in
the shadows
kisses venom.

Sleeps between
my love and I
in our bed.

Conjurer
Oh Conjurer,

Hidden hand
of spoken thought
and whispered prayer

come erase
to the space between
now and forever
lest this unseen
castle fails
to disappear.

Evelyn Nesbit

All is God
the kiss
the curse

the whispered prayer
the hammered trigger.

Death is
an invitation
beyond the
parted curtain,
an orchestra pit.

Life in
stages.

We are an audience
of actors applauding
our own reflections.

One must die
many times
on many stages
before she lives
to see
the script.

Rottweiler Choir

This NGH died
for something.

I don't go
for old age.

I don't go
for disease.

I say
murder.

Which poets die
of natural causes?

Which poems kill?

I saw the
rifles pointed.

Jesse Jackson with
that blood on his shirt.

"BarakaBarakaBarakaBaraka!"

Pitbull orchestra.
Rottweiler choir.

Monk on an "expression-scriber."

Sometimes, pianos
make better sense
of trees than trees
themselves.

Charlie Parker, what you say?
"A typewriter is corny!"

This is a stick-up.

Amiri, get out of the coffin.

I saw you
dancing on
Langston's ashes.

They raised the bounty
on Assata's head
and called it "inflation."

Lying-in-state
of New Jersey.

Washington,
cross the Delaware.

Gov'nor,
stop up
the bridge.

We can't let
this poet's spirit
get out.

Dearly beloved,
We are gathered here today
to get through this thing called life.

Even death
is a part of life.

Either this is a funeral
or the senate floor.

We all knew
the politicians
would show up.

We gon' Lo-ku
the twitterverse.

God as a male model
who frequented
the World Trade bathroom.

Neither God
could have made this up.

Neither God.

Neither God.

Somebody said Jesus
got caught at the border.

I say, if you let Lazarus fly
Amiri get up and walk.

Can't go out like that.

American culture
is televisonal.

Time to
conceptualize

a series.

The good news is
half of America was
waiting for u to die
in order to read u.

BOOM

an eagle
flying over Harlem
as I write this.

NGH I'm not even makin' this up.

Riverside Drive.

Brown-tipped.
Now, leaning on a light post.

An old game
for eagles

posing for anthems
and poems.

The New York Times
ain't exactly caught up.

Shot him down
in a polarizing vortex.

Amiri Baraka
was no centrist

unless u count
right between
the eyes.

ARIA:
You think I'm crazy?

AH:
I think you're special. I think you're gifted. I think you're connected to a part of yourself most of us ignore. Have you heard from the gallery?

ARIA:
September thirteenth.

Ah's class.

AH:
. . . and one of its forefathers, Afrika Bambaataa, saw that as an opportunity to heighten the information channeled through the medium. So he called on the most famous and most revered rappers of that era, sat them in the same room, and imparted what is now known as the Infinity Lessons. Basically, he said, "Look. We've got all these kids listening. If we stop rapping about partying and

start rapping about
black power, black
history . . . , we can
cover the ground that
school is missing.

So suddenly we have
groups like Boogie
Down Productions,
Public Enemy, Queen
Latifah, The Jungle
Brothers, and BOOM, in
an instant, rap music
shifts from being
simply party music to
now becoming music
that is strategically
aimed to empower.
1987.

All right, five minutes.

Ah puts a mix of '87–'89 hip-hop while he steps outside. American Spirit
loose tobacco in hand.

Cut to:
Aria's room.
Aria painting a red swirling circle in the bottom left corner of a canvas.
Close on Aria writing "Harmonic Convergence" over the circle.

Cut to:
Ah back in class.
Aura Purple raises her hand.

AURA:
My mother always
says my oldest brother

is special because
he was born in 1987.
And that that was the
year of something
called the "Harmonic
Convergence." It's
when something like
five planets aligned and
hippies and new agers
called it the mark of
the ending of history,
twenty-five years before
the end of the Mayan
calendar, 2012, when
the Technosphere
dissolves into the
Nosphere . . . Anyway,
that happened in 1987.

AH:
(making an appeal
to a few distracted
students)
Well, wait guys. Let's
say Afrika Bambaataa's
Soulsonic Force
takes its importance
because it incorporates
Pythagoras's "music of
the spheres" into the
mix, which by nature
makes it "anthemic."
Let's say that without it,
the women and children,
the most susceptible,
the most open, the most
vulnerable, would not

be as open to the forces
of music or, let alone,
the forces of planetary
transience of the
Harmonic Convergence
or . . .

How He Talks to Me

Answer me.

If I hadn't come

If I hadn't doubted
Worried, feared,
Lost my way

If I hadn't have kissed you

If none of this were real
If it all had no meaning
If my prayers were in vain

If integrity were nothing,
More than a branch of the ego
And dreams just an excuse we use
to escape the eternally real:
pain, suffering, death, betrayal

If all that was good
was simply a lie

would this moment feel any different?

Here

Now

Your body so close
I feel the sweat of your pores
Entering mine

And this kiss? And this?

Would this then be heaven? Love?

Listen, every dream does come true
if you hold it close.

And there is a boundary
Beyond which ego cannot persist.

I want you to come with me.

If you cannot walk, let me carry you.

I want to show you what I have found.

A dream I had as a child has blossomed
Into a castle. You can have your own wing,
Although, I doubt you will need it.

My love, your dreams have blossomed too.
And all that is missing from their sacred grove
Is you.

Come.

Without you a garden becomes
a vacant lot. A castle: a nutshell.

It appears you've lost your map.

Let me draw one on your belly.
And, here, on your thigh.

It will all be clear
when the paint dries.

Closer to Birth Than I Am to Death

Birth,

a false beginning.

We are here
all along.

Death, an example
of the end

that is not.

Le Poisson Rouge

You will remember me.

How I stood at the face of the mountain,
warmed by a fire I had not known to exist.

Swallowed by history.
Betrothed to the future.

I am my afterlife.
I am my son.

I live beyond breath,

speak beyond tongue.

Subharmonic Matrix.

Mercurial mask.

Yield to the undertow.

Fish in a flask.

AH cont':
Wait. Won't we all agree
that the current and
ocean flow is dictated
by the moon? The most
ancient calendars,
Hebrew, Chinese, and
even Mayan, I believe,
are all dictated by
the moon. The lunar
calendars—which is
to say that the grid
of twenty-eight days,
making thirteen full or
new moons in a year—
has been accepted
through time as a
calculable assessment
of cyclical change, both
in nature and humanity,
which is to say, in life
Itself.
Yet, here we all stand
two-thousand odd years
from the birth of Christ,
on an uneven grid that
labels the number
thirteen evil, living by
a calendar dictated
by the church, which
divorces us from feeling
any synchronicity with
nature or the moment,
because we are
consumed by machine
and minute, the cross
and clock. We work nine

to five. Even slavery was the taking of those who lived on one of these so called "primitive" calendars and putting them on the clock, the standard, the grid, the box. So my question to you is

Minimizing, Denying, and Blaming

The silent "b"
in doubt and debt
mutates our right
to b.

They crave control
of how we think
of how we feel and see.

We learn
to pronounce
mystery as mastery and fail
to understand
that even
within fate
is the power
of the will

If freedom
needs a sanctuary
history needs
a cell

with bars
to keep
its hands
from reaching
out beyond
what mothers tell
their young.

We are
songs
unsung.

Hit or Miss

Every enemy
of every me

bleeding
through
this pen.

Every soul
that cowers
weak
when faced
with a new friend.

Everything
we know
of doubt
is time

divided
by the Sun.

Every living testament
extinguished by the gun.

Minstrel

All my life
I have waited
for this moment.

Years of rehearsal.

Dress rehearsals
and run-throughs.

Lost myself
in the process.

Made wrong choices.

Often felt
there was
no choice.

The stage.

The lights.

The anticipation.

But now it is
opening night.

The audience
has begun to take
their seats

And soon, love,
so soon it will be time

to part the curtains.

AH cont':
could your doubt in the
connection between the
Harmonic Convergence
that Aura has introduced
us to and the Golden
Age of Hip-Hop, the
coming of age of a
generation, and perhaps
a society, particularly
in 1987, be connected
to the fact that we
have all quite literally
been programmed by
the manufacturers of
time and divorced from
nature and cycle to
doubt the relationship
between time and
space? To doubt history
as mystery?

The class breaks into spontaneous applause and laughter. Ah laughs
too.

AH:
And, once again, we're
out of time . . .

Students begin to filter out. Aura stays behind. As she stands, we notice
that she is quite pregnant.

AH:
How are you holding up,
Ms. Purple?

AURA:
Good.

AH:
I think you answered
a question I had today.
If your mom's a hippie
then Aura Purple is more
than likely your real
name.

AURA:
Yep. I have a question
for you Mr. . . . Ah,
it's about the dream
assignment. I'm happy
to do it, but I don't really
see its connection to
the stuff we discuss in
class.

AH:
(chuckles)
Neither do I, Aura, but
I'm trying to figure it out.

Aura chuckles and begins to walk away.

AH:
Aura, when are you due?

AURA:
September thirteenth.

Love and the Mountaineer

Have we ever
thanked the moon
for mountains?

Shifts   in current
create   shifts in land mass
beneath   the sea. These shifts in
land   mass push the fault lines
'til we   are perched on breathless.
It is   the moon that shifts the
current   that restarts it all.

Love is funny.

Sometimes it farts
to save a moment
from becoming
more than it should be

decides
when a kiss
can shift
a season.

It is within us

and it breathes
how we breathe

and it smiles
how you smile

and it laughs
when I write
about it.

Untitled

How to tame an ego
when it wilds
to compare?

Am I all
that she thinks
of me?

Am I less
than my share?

I share fears.

I share expertise.

I share most
of my love.

I am shy
about some of it.

I ball fists
beneath gloves.

I am hidden
in open space.

I am kind
by design.

I am kindling
in burning flames.

Untitled.

Unsigned.

Stephen Torton Kicks Off His Shoes

Lightweight Symphony.

Dance of the brave.

Desperate dignity.

Daze of the crazed.

Do what you wanna do.

Say what you please.

Downright diggity.

Blend in and freeze.

What would Basquiat do?

a. Throw some D's on it?

b. Put Adidas and Lee's on it?

c. Write "copyright"
   and pee on it?

d. All of the above.

Patient as death
holds its spoon to Great Love.

Voices
like graffiti

tag thoughts
bomb minds.

Noises
of the city
airports
long lines.

Choices
by committee.
Years taught.
Designed.

Poised
For the pity.

Un-poised
for the find.

VNDRZ was blind.

The History of Self Defense

Okay—

       Let's say

              there's a man.

A wish-horse

          a wanderer.

          Let's say that he is your friend.

              Let's say this man
              has *tendencies*.

          Sings more than he speaks.

             Dabbles in mastery.

           Let's say he's a leader

           un-warriored and pure.
           Mangled in mercury
           marveled by math.

          Let's say he is an only child

              though siblings
              grace his chart.

              Let's say he prefers
              make-believe.

Sees science in his art.

Now what does
"make-believe"
mean to you?

Not real? Fictitious?
Imaginary? In the mind?

Distinguish this
from dreams.

Distinguish from God.

Now back
　　　　to the man.

Back? Why back?

Stay in place.

Let's say this man has wings.

Let's say this man
can walk in place

and glides through everything.

Let's say
this man
has chosen
　　　sides.

Let's say

that he
rebels

against the norm
prefers the storm

and rhymes when
meanings swell.

Would you rather
he paint your chapel?

Would he rather
build a chair?

Would you rather
give him pen and pad
to calculate the air?

Would you bid him
lead an army?

Would you give him
a guitar?

Would you offer
him a place to sleep?

A blanket and a meal?

Would u trust him
where your children sleep?

Would u teach them
how to kill?

Would you trust this man
with precious gifts
bestowed through
nature's will?

The history of Self Defense
was seldom writ in stone.

The priests who
kept their secrets close
believed in flowing robes
and in them stored metallurgy

of currency and cross
to pick through stone and sever bone of bulls,
of rams, of goats . . .

Aria appears in the doorway.

                                        AH:
                                        Aria! Hey, what are you
                                        doing here?

A strange moment of recognition as Aura and Aria pass each other. Aura
exits.

                                        ARIA:
                                        I just had to get out of
                                        the house. I wanted to
                                        see you.

Ah and Aria embrace.

                                        AH:
                                        You okay? What
                                        happened?

                                        ARIA:
                                        I kept dreaming. They
                                        threw me off of the ship.
                                        They . . .

                                        AH:
                                        They threw you off the
                                        ship? Wait. Come on.
                                        Let's get out of here.

                                        ARIA:
                                        I want coffee.

City street. Day
Ah and Aria walking down the street. Ah is walking his bike. Aura has
coffee.

ARIA:

It felt like knowing a
recipe that's handed
down but was actually
never told to you. I say
my name three times
and I drop like I'm
dead . . . but I'm not
dead. And everyone else,
or mostly everyone else
that's dropped dead on
the ship, aren't dead
either. But they pile us
on top of each other,
on the deck. Everyone.
Everyone that has
somehow gotten the
message to say their
own names three times
in a row. And can feel
their bodies next to
mine. We're not dead.
But, me, I'm scared to
death, because I heard
that if you die in your
dream then you die. But
I can't wake up. Not in
the dream. Not from the
dream. And they throw
us off the ship, all of **us**,
undead. And no one's
waking up. And we're
floating. And the ship
sails out of the picture.

AH:
I can't talk you into
getting a water bed
then, eh?

ARIA:
Shut up, Ah.

Ah walks his bike up the steps of their building. He walks into the front
room and sees "Harmonic Convergence" written across the canvas.
Ah freezes. He sits silently on the couch across from the painting,
dumbfounded.

Aria receives a text as she enters.

ARIA:
I gotta go. Baby? Ah?

Ah is staring at the painting.

ARIA:
You okay?

AH:
Who put that there?

ARIA:
What do you mean?
It's what I woke up
with this morning,
before I came to see
you. What? You okay?

AH:
Wow. I'm okay. We
talked about this in class

today. . . . I know, you
gotta go. It's okay.

There's a knock on the door. Ah snaps out of his trance and heads toward
the door.

Choose a Side

One sided argument
greedy and corpulent
suffering sycophant
tortured and dissident
reckless the incumbent
angry and indolent
unfed, the indigent
knowledgeably ignorant
bothered and negligent

Skull and bones
cranial instruments

give me my

      me my

   me my paintings back.

     You'll have to pay for them.

      Cash and prizeless
      ashes and lotion
      water and oil
      handfuls of soil

      excrement
      dirt of life
      breadfruit and albatross
      cartons of light

      oxygenesis

manpower vs. horsepower

Atlas Shrugged

Fruit of my labor

web of my worth and
worthlessness

First son
      of capitalism

Master Teacher

Sensei

Messiah

Handprints
      and silver arms

Look through your eye.
A planet
with rings

black eyes

translucence.

Doubtless in the All.

Paint schools
orange and yellow.

Uncolor the hydrants.

Water your weapons.

Dance for me.

Reject your chosen bride.

I will choose for you

crash the waves for you

embrace them as they rise.

Green leaves
in the sunlight.

Blasphemy

blank-face

no expression.

Explain it to me.
Make sense of it.
Choose a side.

The Mars Volta Live in Charleston

Because the rocket's red glare
blinded ancestors but did not
deafen ears to the sound of
truths come back to haunt
the desolate mansions of
our manhood.

Because songs of the railroad
will be sung 'til iron bends in
the grasp of freedom.

Because one man's story
is the story of many.

Mythic folklore of the future
deciphered by those who dare.

Because the answers to every
question ever posed sits numb
before the camera knowing
a flash of light cannot fathom
its essence.

Because the laughter of our
generation will pierce the crying
souls of Vieques and El Paso, of
those who cannot forget the Alamo,
nor the creeping hands of the
Confederacy.

> And when this
> chalk outline circles our city
> we will conjure that mythic strength
> and return to the drawing board and

each village and commune will take
the name of a made-up story,

handwritten by
the children of survivors.

Montage

Oh beautiful
for spacious skies
where land
is misbegotten.

The fallen lumber
of the mind.

Harvests
chemically
rotten.

The purple swell
of majesty
now utters
the downtrodden.

Where beef
is sold
a million fold.

Where hands bled
for the cotton.

Tobacco fields with interest
yields what free thought
lost through chimneys.

Where flags were laid
across the graves dug
in the minds of plenty.

Where once was taught
the cost of war now sold
from every TV.

Song Keeper

Philosophical treatises over music
through and around it: harmonic
epiphany.

Sound as the soft-tongued
server. Hard-edged. Corrupt.

What is a corrupt sound?

What is a breakbeat?
A sample?

Mixed media.
White noise.

Strength in repetition.

Omission. O mission!

The glory of vision.
Mirrors. Reflectors.

Translucent transparency.

The Pharaoh's
inner Pharisee.

Discordant fallacy:

You can't dance to this.

Only kill. And dissolve.

Violent Disharmony.

Only time can absolve.

What is silence?

Answer me.

What is it with you poets
and free thinkers?

Why do you keep
trying to baffle me?

What is this twisted tongue?

What can it speak of
that I have not already heard?

He stood in paint
splattered boots

uncrossed his arms

and looked at me.

"I can tell you
what silence is."

"It is the answer
of the wind
in response
to the question
wings ask."

"Every letter
of your alphabet
is an instrument."

"The O's are
the mouths of horns
obviously."

He laughed
before intensifying
his stare.

"Booom. Booom."

This NGH's crazy,
I thought. Leave
it to me to get stuck
with the weird NGH
in the room. Rooooom.

I searched around
quickly for someone
I recognized.

He stood still,
dimmed his
smiling eyes,
and said to me,

"Your thoughts
are the loudest
thing in the room."

"Your heart
has 'om' within
    its boom."

"Your breath
like rivers flow

through lungs."

"Yet, every thought
will share one tongue."

"Do you determine
which thoughts
you voice or do they
determine you?"

Your head
like a fish tank
that fish
swim through.

Each fish
is an "I"
you let speak
for you.

When will you
become an observer?

When will you
garden your ability
to discern between
what is taught and
what one could teach?

What is the freedom
you exercise through
speech?

Say What You Feel

A swirling of energy
soundless and still.

Type in the vestibule.
Jump brooms and sills.

Sultan of sandy shore.
Falcon of hills.

Compounded
to cement.

The dulling of drills.

All is nil.

All is nil.

Say what u feel.

Songbird of the Unworded Testament

Voices through darkness
erase the mystery.

No drumbeat
is heartless.

Tongue pierced
by history.

Back strong
as liberty.

My skin is
transparent

it's the blood
that you see.

Nectar of godless angels.

Descendants of
the Evermore

Maximizing
existence
through song.

Enchanting blood
to sing along.

Songbird of the unworded testament

This is a voice
given for you.

Likewise the cup
also, following:

Sarah, Billie, Bessie,
Ella, Mahalia, Nina

gathered
at a table
sipping wine

The last supper
before yet another.

Offering everything
for the price of cotton,
hard labor, abuse,
a cool sip of reefer,
a night in somebody's arms,
a kiss like a muted trumpet.

Listen closely and you will hear
your mother's name.

Okri walks in holding a beautifully distressed wooden door.

> **AH:**
> (liking what he sees)
> Yo!

> **OKRI:**
> Yo, someone threw it out
> around the corner.

> **ARIA:**
> (on her way out):
> Wow. That's beautiful.
> Okay, love. I'll check in
> later.

Aria exits.

> **AH:**
> Let's take that up.

Cut to:

Ah and Okri on the rooftop. Ah is finishing his ship adding new doors, odds
and ends, found objects, car windows, and street signs.

> **OKRI:**
> It wows me.

> **AH:**
> What?

> **OKRI:**
> Everything, every
> moment that anyone
> allows themselves to be
> taken for granted. I was
> cast as Prince Hal in
> *Henry IV* today.

AH:
Congrats.

OKRI:
Well, yeah, it dawns
on me that history is
make-believe. I'll do
my best to embody
the emotional depth
of this character for
the sake of conveying
something that *is.* And if
the audience chooses to
believe it, it will not be
about them attaining a
better grasp on history,
but really about them
catching glimpses of
themselves, here and
now. It's just a tool to
illuminate the moment.
We shine a spotlight on
a chosen few to make
sense of what lies in the
shadows. Us.

AH:
Those thrown
overboard . . .

OKRI:
What?

AH:
*Those thrown overboard
had overheard
the mysteries of
the undertow and*

understood that down
below there would be no
more chains.

OKRI:
What's that?

AH:
. . . a possibility.

Still Life

Our father
who art in darkness,
shallow be thy grave.

Thy kingdom done.
Thy will re-hung.

On Earth
there is no heaven.

Give us this day
our daily dead.

And forgive us
the trespassers
who dare to dream
beyond it.

Our guns
and our temptations
deliver every evil.

Our mind is the kingdom.
Each thought holds its power.
We bask in Old Glory.

Forever and ever,

no end.

Harmonic Convergence

Words and worlds converge. Red streaks across the screen. We zoom in on the words until the words disappear. Ultra-magnetic. Divine Styler. Lava rises to fill the screen then shoots up and over it. Red glaze on a snow globe. Within the globe are people living, working, on a mountainside, the side of a volcano. An old muscular woman is ceremoniously placed in what appears to be an oversized black coffin, which is standing upright, like a bass case. A large door is opened on the side of the mountain, smooth and solid like an organic bank vault. Within the door is a passageway to another door. Beyond this door, a pool of lava. The woman is pushed using a rolling platform. The encasement descends into lava. The three doors are closed and sealed shut. Outside there are hundreds surrounding the base of the mountain. The sky is molten red with windows to the sea. Coral drums and hums converge with the sounds of the whales and dolphins. The people move gracefully, as if freed by water.

On land, the rain begins.

(c.)

Sketches of L'Héroïne

MAY 1954. Harlem, New York City.
HOTEL AMERICA. DAY.
A cut up of nondescript images over an ambient distortion of sounds in the key of F. A fetus. A man's nipple. The mouth of a horn. Finger tips. A tongue. A black cat. A spider web. The silhouette of the feet of a hanging man. The sole of a tap dancer's foot.

We are close on the eyes of Miles Davis.
His pupils are dilated. He stares into a mirror, softly speaking a melody to himself.

> **MILES:**
> Rain, rain, down pour—
> Dreams.

Miles is speaking in a pitched staccato. He elongates the final word, like holding a high and arching note ("Dreeeeeeaaaaaaaams").

> **MILES:**
> Rain, rain, down pour—
> Dreams.
> Hello. Hello. Hello. Hello.
> Hello. Hello . . .

He repeats the word as if in an echo chamber.

> **MILES (V.O.):**
> I was fucked, man. I had
> seen it in other cats'
> eyes, but never in my
> own. You can see it.

Clear as day. And you
think, "man, if I could
see like this all the
time . . ."

Bright, mid-afternoon.
Miles is standing in the bathroom of a bare, nondescript hotel room in
Harlem. T-shirt and ruffled pants. He looks like he hasn't slept.

> **MILES (V.O.):**
> and it ain't that you
> ain't seen like that
> before, it's more like
> *this* is how you can
> see like that *all the
> time.* . . . Yeah, man. I
> had my own logic and
> reasoning and shit had
> just come down to it.

Miles walks towards the window to the bed and begins to lift his trumpet
from its case before noticing the tie wrapped around his forearm.

The sign slightly visible through the far window reads "Hotel America."

> **MILES (V.O.):**
> I can't say it made my
> playing any better. And
> I can't say that's what
> made me try it in the
> first place.

Miles unties the tie from his arm and grabs his jacket from beside the
trumpet. He notices a bird flying by the window.
Handwritten sheets of music are strewn across the room.

MILES (V.O.):
A lot of cats I knew
became junkies trying
to sound like Bird. But
I had spent too much
time flying with Bird to
try to sound like him. I
was busy developing my
own sound.

Miles puts his jacket on before noticing his shirt crumpled beside the toilet.

MILES (V.O.):
Just like I had developed
my own habit.

Miles walks back to the bathroom, picks up his shirt and looks back in the mirror.

We are back on the eyes of Miles Davis as he stares inquisitively at himself, dazed.

We hear the slow drip of the faucet from the sink beneath him. When Miles looks down to inspect, the slow drip turns in to a slow stream—the sound of someone peeing.

MILES (V.O.):
Juliette.

Miles glances over and sees a dark-haired, olive skin, Juliette Greco. She's naked, sitting on the toilet, and smiling mischievously up at Miles with big black eyes.

MILES (V.O.):
If you wanna know
about getting high or
feelin high—like us,
sitting around this fire
telling stories—the first
time I felt it, it wasn't
no drug. It was music. It
was a woman.

(voices of a small group of men, laughing)

Miles does a slow blink, a double-take and she's gone.

MILES (V.O.):
I was haunted.

The toilet is bare. We hear the drip from the faucet. He splashes water on his face and looks deeply into his own eyes.

MILES (V.O.):
Heroin was just a
mattering of the fact.
And the fact was that I
couldn't fight the feeling.

Miles continues his staccato melody into the mirror, softly, maintaining the same rhythm as before.

MILES:
French. Witch. Bitch.
Voodoooooooooo . . .

Miles does one more take in the mirror. He closes his eyes and when he opens them, we are peering through a glass window—as if on the other side of the mirror—as he continues to stare straight out.

MILES (V.O.):
If you was in my head,
mostly what you'd hear
would be music. Maybe
something you never
heard before.

Lights streak across the glass and Miles' face.

MILES (V.O.) cont':
I heard music
everywhere. Heroin just
turn't the mothafucka
up.

His look is focused, yet dazed. Intense. He is sitting in the backseat of a
taxi driving over a bridge. We are moving at the same speed as the car.

The sound of the tires crossing the steel grids of the bridge is loud and
rhythmic.

MILES (V.O.) cont':
In the streets, in the
lights and colors, in
the wind, in the way a
woman moves . . .

Over his shoulders, we notice a blond woman, crouched, facing the wrong
direction, passionately kissing a man who is seated beside Miles in the
back of the taxi.

MILES (V.O.) cont':
And I was moving, full
speed ahead. Sitting
beside the pilot.

The man—30s, brown complexioned, in an ill-fitted suit—is vacillating between kissing the woman and eating a piece of chicken. The man goes from kissing the woman's lips to biting the chicken, as if it is all part of the act.

> **MILES (V.O.) cont':**
> Charlie Parker. Bird.
> The mouthpiece of our
> organization.

The man—Bird—begins biting and licking the chicken, more suggestively, as the woman crouches further down between his legs.

> **MILES (V.O.):**
> Pilot of inner-freedom
> through reckless
> abandon. Genius didn't
> discriminate.

Miles adjusts himself in the cramped space and turns angrily to address Charlie Parker:

> **MILES:**
> Come on, Bird.

> **BIRD:**
> Aw Miles, if you don't
> like it, put your head
> out the mothafuckin'
> window.

Miles turns away disgustedly, and begins to roll down the window.

> **MILES (V.O.) cont':**
> And even a greedy pig

like him was a different
story with a sax in his
mouth.

Miles puts on a pair of black shades and peers out the window just as the descending glass is crossing the threshold of his eyes.

MILES (V.O.) cont':
So what the fuck is you
lookin' at?

We notice the eyes of the taxi driver peering through the rearview mirror.

MILES (V.O.):
It was the first time
I became aware of
mothafuckas looking
at me like I had some
disease. With pity

The mood picks up as the sound of drums begins to play along with the sound of the tires crossing the steel grids.

Miles puts his entire head out the window.

MILES (V.O.) cont':
The problem was, it
wasn't the first time
a NGH had stuck his
head out the window in
disgust and discovered
wind.

Heavy wind and the clang of the tires, loop into a rhythm. The drums solo around it.

Miles's face is close to the camera.

The lights collide off of the reflected lens of Miles's shades, like a light painting, fireworks. The colors streak in yellow, blue and white.

TITLE: L'HEROINE

MILES (V.O.) cont':
Yeah. In that sense, I guess you could say I was high.

We pan out to the immense skyline of Manhattan. The checkered cab is just one of the many stories on the Queensboro Bridge at night. The lights and skyline of Manhattan shine brilliantly and in contrast to the large steel grids of the bridge.

A voice scatting a fast melody over the drums.

The feet of a man tap dancing on the sidewalk outside of a club, as the taxi pulls up. Miles, head still out the window, is watching the dancer.

MILES:
You hear that? Tttttt. . . .

A percussive shuffling rhythm picks up where the tires' sound leaves off—seamless.

MILES (V.O.):
What Bird and Dizzy had played together had broken the sound-barrier.

The dancer is voicing his steps like a quick-paced horn solo: ("Trinkle Tinkle.")

MILES (V.O.):
Now, Bird's father was a
tap dancer.

He's dancing directly towards another man standing in the fold: his challenger. People are gathered around watching.

The sign outside the club reads: MINTON'S PLACE.

MILES (V.O.):
The tap dancers were
timekeepers, putting
their own signature on
time and the times.

Miles exits the car, as Bird and the woman exit from the other side. Miles stands on the curb, transfixed by the dancer.

MILES (V.O.):
Maybe we watched how
they hoofed between the
beats and imitated them
in our horn solos.

Miles watches the dancers feet as they step perfectly with the fast paced melody.

MILES (V.O.):
Maybe they imitated us.

Miles notices two very well-dressed black men who are shaking hands with Bird while looking at the tap dancers, like they've bet money on them.

> **MILES (V.O.) cont':**
> We were like miners
> with them lights on our
> hats . . .

One of the well-dressed men reaches discreetly into his suit pocket and hands Bird something.

> **MILES (V.O.) cont':**
> . . . looking for gold and
> faster ways of finding it.

Bird slides money under his palm. The well-dressed man keeps his eyes on the dancer.

> **MILES (V.O.) cont':**
> And that gold was
> something we injected
> pure into our ears.

The dancer moves with brutal intensity. Another dancer looks on, not impressed.

(**Voices:** "Come on, Lefty." "All right now.")

Miles approaches the well-dressed men and makes the same transaction as Bird.

> **MILES (V.O.) cont':**
> Bebop was that—before
> it was commercial.

A well-dressed white couple pull up in a taxi and walk hurriedly into the club.

MILES (V.O.) cont':
White people had
already run off with
what they called "jazz."
But they couldn't take
what they couldn't
imitate.

The second tap dancer, in the spirit of competition, jumps in, voicing a different fast-paced melody that matches his graceful footwork. ("Donna Lee.") The first dancer relents.

MILES (V.O.) cont':
Bebop was that before
it was exploited—it was
a way of preparing a
drug—a faster way of
getting high.

A young, lean, distinguished man watches Miles from behind.

MILES (V.O.) cont':
Those double-time
tempos and riffs weren't
for everybody. It was
personal.

The man taps his shoulder. Miles jumps.

MILES (V.O.) cont':
And being a black man
in America kept a NGH
on his toes.

MAX:
(worried)
Hey, Miles. You all right?

Miles is embarrassed.

MILES:
Max.

MAX:
(decides to hide
his worry. Acts like
everything's okay.)
You look good, Miles.

He slides a folded bill into Miles's front pocket.

Max, inside, playing the drums we've been hearing since the bridge.

MILES (V.O.):
I was fucked, but I was
fucking with the time-
keepers who kept time
by setting it free.

An old piano player stamps his foot wildly, as he plays.

MILES (V.O.) cont':
Look at his foot.

The audience is a wide array of uptown sophistication, at tables and the
bar.

Miles slow-motion walking into the club. Through the open door we see a
police car drive by, slowly, with its window down.

MILES (V.O.) cont':
I ain't no historian, but I think it says something about how we could outmaneuver our white masters who thought we was stupid.

The cops look disapprovingly at the assembled crowd and dancers as they pass.

MILES (V.O.) cont':
Most of America was behind the times.

Miles approaches the stage just as Bird walks out of the shadows. They begin playing at the same time, a jagged fast-paced melody.

MILES (V.O.):
Bebop built time machines. And in May 1949, a vortex opened that I had to go through before I arrived on the other side.

The band plays. Max plays a thousand beats in a movement. Bird flies over the music. Miles does a slow blink and when he opens his eyes . . .

Miles is back in his bathroom in the Hotel America—his head leaning against the bathroom mirror.

MILES (V.O.):
I was fucked.

                                        MILES:
                                        (Singing his staccato
                                        melody.)
                                        Rain, rain, down pour—
                                        Dreams.

There is a knock at the hotel room door. Miles hears a familiar male voice
outside.

                                        VOICE AT DOOR:
                                        Miles? Miles? You in
                                        there?

Miles recognizes the voice, his father. His head bows in shame.

                                        MILES (V.O.) cont':
                                        And word had evidently
                                        gotten home.

                                        MILES' FATHER:
                                        Come on, son. I know
                                        you're in there. Open up.

He walks slowly towards the door.

The passing countryside as Miles rides, nervously, in a car with his father.

Miles is staring out the window.

                                        MILES (V.O.):
                                        Saint Louis wasn't
                                        Harlem.

The green flora of trees. Arkansas.

MILES (V.O.):
Harlem wasn't Paris.
America wasn't France.

What looks like a man hanging from a tree catches Miles's attention.

MILES (V.O.) cont':
And once I saw it clearly,
I tried to stay as high as
possible, if only to float
over the bullshit.

A bird flies close and over the car. Miles watches it closely.

MILES (V.O.):
I floated over racism. I
floated over injustice.
I floated over
responsibility.

Miles through the window of a plane flying over the Atlantic.

MILES (V.O.) cont':
I floated over the ocean.

MILES POV: Through the window are just a few clouds in a blue sky.

On the foldout tray in front of him, Miles drawing lines across paper, and then a few small circles, between the lines: a miniature sketch of the sky outside: whole notes.

MILES (V.O.):
I floated through music.

Images of fighter planes bombarding Paris, made to look like postcards.

MILES (V.O.):
I floated back to Paris.

Blackbirds flailing in slow motion around the head of a woman on a Paris street. She is dark haired with big eyes, staring up at the birds as they fly close and around her head.

Juliette stares directly into camera.

MILES (V.O.) cont':
Do you believe in signs?

Miles standing in front of the mirror of a dark room as he removes the clothes he had on in the car. He looks sick, disheveled. There is a made bed in what appears to be an old wooden shack. Small beams of light pierce through cracks in the walls and the closed shutters of the window.

Miles stumbles toward the window. When he opens the shutters . . .

Hotel La Louisiane Saint-Germain-des-Prés, Paris. May 1949.
A well-dressed, clean-cut Miles opens the window of his hotel room.

On the street, the sidewalk cafe, outside the hotel is lively. People are seated at tables. Morning traffic on the street.

A flock of birds swoop by.

The voice of Bessie Smith is coming from a nearby window.

MILES (V.O.):
What the fuck do you
believe in?

Miles picks up his horn and begins to play, softly over the music.

Miles sees Max and Moody exit the hotel and greet an excited young Frenchman.

In real time, Miles puts his trumpet in its case and adjusts his tie and hair in the mirror.

On the other side of the wall, Juliette is in the mirror applying mascara. Bessie Smith is at full volume playing off a phonograph on the floor of her room.

Miles exits his room just as a young black man exits his room a few doors down.

> **MAN:**
> (to Miles)
> Hey, man.

> **MILES:**
> Hey.

Outdoor cafe terrace.
Miles and the young man approach Max and Moody, who are seated at a table. The man is frail, effeminate, casually dressed, and wears his hair "conked" like Miles.

> **MAX:**
> Miles!

> **MILES:**
> Hey y'all—this is Jimmy.
> I caught him listening to
> Bessie Smith upstairs.

Max and James Moody laugh.

> **MILES:**
> Says he's been living in
> Paris for a year. Must
> have been homesick.

Jimmy is elegant in his gestures and greetings. Instantly likable.

Jimmy sits.

> **JIMMY:**
> So we having a Minton's
> revival here in Paris
> tonight?

Smiles.

> **MAX:**
> Where you from man?

> **JIMMY:**
> Harlem.

> **MAX:**
> And you live over here?

Jimmy nods.

> **MOODY:**
> So what you doing for
> bread?

> **MAX:**
> Yeah, what do you play?

JIMMY:
(laughs)
I play the typewriter.

MOODY:
I knew you was a writer.

MILES:
Man, you look like you
can tap!

More laughs.

MILES:
You ain't no music critic,
is you?

MOODY:
Must be something, eh?
It ain't like home over
here.

JIMMY:
No, it's something
different. Something that
doesn't call you boy or
nigger. It don't stop the
ghosts from circling,
but the ghosts got their
own ghosts and ghost
writers . . .

A young energetic Frenchman approaches the table and addresses Miles.

BORIS:

Excuse me sir. Would
you like to buy a
trumpet? It's full of life.
Hasn't been to bed with
too many men . . .

MILES:

. . .

Boris laughs and breaks character.

BORIS:

Ah, Mr. Davis. I'm
sorry. It's a bad joke.
I'm Boris, your liaison
here—Welcome in
Paris. If you give me the
music sheets for Donna
Lee you can have the
trumpet.

MILES:

That trumpet's a piece
of shit. What I need your
trumpet for?

BORIS:

Oh, excuse me, Mr.
Davis.

MILES:

(laughing)
Nah, it's a bad joke. Yeah,
I'll write it down for you.
What you mean, now?

                                    BORIS:
                                    Yes. I have a concert
                                    tonight at the Salle
                                    Pleyel.

The guys laugh.

                                    MILES:
                                    Get ahold of this
                                    motherfucker.

                                    BORIS:
                                    Fine, I'll wait.

Boris winks and walks away, speaking directly to camera. (italics =
French)

                                    BORIS:
                                    *I may be just a
                                    "wingman" dans cette
                                    histoire. But this is my
                                    wing. The wing of a
                                    blackbird swallowed
                                    whole by a black cat.
                                    Saint-Germain-des-Prés,
                                    Paris, 1949.*

Boris approaches a table at the cafe where an older bespectacled man, a
middle-aged woman and a younger blond woman sit.

                                    **THE BLOND
                                    WOMAN:**
                                    Boris!

BESPECTACLED MAN:
Up rather early this morning.

MIDDLE-AGED WOMAN:
The Festival. Dizzy. What magnificent names.

BORIS:
Yes, the musicians have just arrived.

The blonde stands up to leave. Boris stops her.

BORIS:
Have you seen Toutoune? Any news?

BLONDE:
Oh Boris, it's terrible. She's locked herself in her room. I'm really worried.

BORIS:
She's there now?

BLONDE:
Sí.

BORIS:
I'm gonna go check on her.

Boris walking through the crowd into the hotel lobby, talks direct to camera.

BORIS:

Here are the biggest tits in Europe, gathered in ant-dance formation, lifting oversized pieces of bread to hungry fascist pirates. Don't be deceived by what you see here. Scandal and fascination with scandal is the mother of all media. You could not capture beauty unless you murdered it.

Walking up the steps inside the hotel.

BORIS:

On the other hand, we are here to nurture beauty . . . to conjure it to dance, sing, explore itself. To welcome it out of its self-imposed cage and encourage its nocturnal wanderings. Wanderings? This is awful. Who wrote this? The Controversial American Negro writer Vernon Sullivan once said that there are only two things: love, all

*sorts of love with pretty
girls, and the music
of New Orleans: jazz.
All else is bullshit. SO
what are we going on
about? Saint-Germain
is the home to many
things, existentialist
philosphers, great
literary and dramatic
pioneers, painters,
poets, and . . . and when
jazz comes to visit.*

He knocks on a door.

BORIS:
Blues pour un chat noir.

Juliette opens the door. She is dressed in black. Bessie Smith plays quietly off the phonograph. She is an emotional wreck and immediately breaks upon seeing Boris.

JULIETTE:
Oh Boris.

BORIS:
*Oh ma petite, I'm
confused. I hear the
good news of your role
in Cocteau's film and
find you here mourning?*

JULIETTE:
*Yes, but who have I been
cast to portray? Death!*

There is nothing but
death around me.

Boris laughs.

JULIETTE:
It's not funny. I'm
frightened, Boris. It's
something in the air. I
feel a swooping terror,
legions of black ghosts
crowd me on to swiftly
moving roads, sliced
by sheer horizons,
bleeding.

Boris's eyes glaze over.

BORIS:
Ah, Juliette. We're all
dead and dying. Now is
the time to celebrate our
afterlife.
Come meet my
American friends!
Musicians from
America!

BORIS cont':
(to camera)
And like that two
households, both alike
in dignity, in fair Paris,
where we lay our scene,
A pair of star-cross'd
lovers, which if you with

203

>   *patient ears attend, a*
>   *hero and his heroine.*

The Conversation:
Rehearsal. Salle Playel. Afternoon.
Miles is standing center-stage as Tadd (piano) begins the intro to "Lady Bird."

Boris enters from the back of the auditorium with Juliette.

>   **BORIS:**
>   (dancing erratically in
>   the aisle)
>
>   *There it is again. They*
>   *smuggle it in under their*
>   *nails and then inject*
>   *it into the instrument.*
>   *Precious penicillin.*

Bass, drums, sax, and Miles come in at the same time and join Tadd with
the melody.

>   **BORIS (V.O.):**
>   Is it in our bodies? Is it
>   in space? Is it the year?
>   The alignment of the
>   stars?

The band plays. Juliette looks straight ahead.

Miles solos.

>   **BORIS (V.O.):**
>   I arrived here with
>   her, without warning.
>   You think this is

improvisaton but it is all
written.

At the end of his solo, the band comes to a meandering halt as the
musicians fidget with their instruments.

> **TADD:**
> (at the piano)
> "Don't Blame Me."

Miles never takes his eyes off Juliette, lifts his trumpet and begins the soft
ballad.

Juliette responds playfully. Each phrase played by Miles is a question
directed towards her.

> **JULIETTE:**
> *Yes, I believe in signs.*

Miles plays.

> **JULIETTE:**
> You dare speak of love
> to me?

Miles plays.

> **JULIETTE:**
> If only you could charm
> death into a dream,
> Orphee.

> **BORIS:**
> (to camera)
> *In an American film,*

                                    she'd probably be
                                    blond . . . but she is
                                    Juliette.

Tadd begins a piano solo.

The song ends.

                                    TADD:
                                    (to the musicians)
                                    Man, everything sounds
                                    peachy to me. Let's say
                                    we get something to eat.

Miles has his eye on Juliette. Juliette does not look away.

                                    BORIS:
                                    (to camera)
                                    And he would be
                                    "the wingman" in a
                                    secondary role . . . but
                                    here, in Paris, he is
                                    wingman no more. See
                                    how it all changes?

The band packs up behind Miles.
Boris walks towards the stage.

                                    BORIS:
                                    Hi, Miles.

                                    BORIS:
                                    (to camera)
                                    Lui c'est . . . Miles Davis!

Boris climbs the stage and exits with the musicians.

Miles and Juliette are alone in the auditorium.

Miles walks to the lip of the stage, eyes locked on Juliette.

Juliette walks down the aisle, eyes on Miles's trumpet.

Miles raises the trumpet to his mouth.

Juliette arrives, slowly traces the trumpet with her finger.

Miles lowers the trumpet. Juliette touches his mouth.

She closes her eyes, tilts her head, and leans in, placing her lips directly in front of Miles's, and then is still.

> JULIETTE (V.O.):
> Souffle.

Miles does not move.

She backs slowly from Miles and pulls out a cigarette. She lights it before placing it, gently into Miles's mouth.

Miles inhales. The tip of the cigarette glows fiery red.

He removes the cigarette from his mouth and begins to blow a slow cloud of smoke.

Juliette places her ear to the cloud of smoke.

She places the cigarette in her mouth and hops on the stage beside Miles.

They look out at the auditorium.

Juliette does a slow tilt of her head to the side, lifting her shoulder gently, as if to say: "Well, that didn't take long."

Miles's eyes glaze over.

She hops down and gestures: "Come on. Let's go."

She begins to walk away.

Miles sits holding his trumpet, amused.

Miles squints his eyes and pulls back his head, incredulously, but with humor: "You talking to me?"

Juliette is amused.

Miles begins to tease with his eyes and soft giggles under his breath. He looks down at Juliette's waist, hips, legs, taking a survey. "So this is it? This is what you look like?"

Juliette, feigning shock and maybe disgust, does a small sarcastic spin for Miles to observe her.

When she finishes, she arches her back and hisses like a cat.

> **JULIETTE:**
> sss . . .

> **MILES:**
> fff . . .
> (and then slowly)
> fuck. you.

Juliette looks into Miles's eyes while forming horns with her hands on the side of her head and then slowly moves those horns to Miles head.

Miles smiles.

Juliette gestures with her head: "Let's go."

Miles and Juliette in the rotund of the theater, a small circular space, with wide white columns, a black-and-white floor, and a ceiling that arches into a globe.

Juliette begins circling around the columns.

> **JULIETTE (V.O.):**
> Vous avez volé de nuit,
> comme les merles?
> Vous les avez
> sifflé pour qu'ils
> m'encerclent?

Miles walks to the center and looks up.

Juliette faces Miles.

> **JULIETTE:**
> Juliette.

Miles nods his head slowly, keeping his eyes on Juliette.

> **MILES:**
> Miles.

Juliette kisses Miles.

Miles pulls back from Juliette's mouth and exhales a cloud of smoke.

The camera glides between the columns.

The smoke clears and reveals

Salle Pleyel. Concert. Night.
Miles blowing into his trumpet, onstage with the band.

Boris is sitting, or trying to stay seated, in the audience. He's enraptured by the music.

Beautiful women and men of all shapes and walks of life, fully taken in by the sound. In awe.

The musicians are each in a zone. They look at each other in confident wonder.

Miles walks offstage as the pianist begins a solo.

Juliette is at the stage door.

Miles walks directly to Juliette and kisses her.

Juliette doesn't hold back.

Miles walks back onstage to play just as the piano solo ends.

He lifts his trumpet and brings the song to its glorious end.

The audience has the energy of seeing their home team win at a sporting event.

Cafe Saint-Germain.
People dance wildly to a small band playing swing in the back of an old cavernous club.

Miles and Juliette squeeze through the doorway.

A few people call out "Hey!" to Juliette and Miles as they enter.

Juliette waves, smiles, holding Miles's hand as she leads him in and through the club.

The crowd is so tight that the only way through is by dancing.

Juliette and Miles walking/dancing through the crowd.

A woman grabs Miles's face and kisses him, as he squeezes past.

Juliette pulls Miles so hard, he almost falls.

MILES:
Hey!

Miles's soft "Hey" has a ripple effect. A group of voices call back in response, "Hey" in synch with the music. Another leader takes over "Hey."

Juliette is standing, tight between people, with her chin tucked and two fists up, like a boxer.

Miles looks Juliette in the eye, lifts his chin in defiance, before biting his lower lip and throwing slow motion jabs, to the music.

Their movement has a ripple effect. The people around them begin a "boxers' jitterbug," moving their fists back and forth.

Boris appears, pushes Juliette out of the way and kisses Miles.

Juliette shouts.

JULIETTE:
Hey!

Juliette, Miles and Boris burst into laughter.

The "Hey" continues its ripple effect.

Boris in a boxing stance.

Boris leads Juliette and Miles to a table full of drinks. A bespectacled man sits with a voluptuous blond woman dancing high on the chair beside him.

Juliette greets the man at the table and then formally introduces Miles.

>   **BORIS:**
>   (to camera)
>   Jean-Paul Sartre will be
>   playing Friar Tuck.

A woman walks up behind Juliette and whispers in her ear.

>   **WOMAN:**
>   *I want to meet him.*

>   **JULIETTE:**
>   Anne-Marie.

>   **ANNE-MARIE:**
>   Hello I'm Anne-Marie.
>   Juliette's friend. You
>   were amazing tonight.

>   **MILES:**
>   Thank you. You speak
>   English!

Juliette turns and dances towards the bar.

>   **JP:**
>   Ah, Anne-Marie, *tu
>   parles anglais*?

Anne-Marie smiles.

>   **ANNE-MARIE:**
>   A little.

>   **JP:**
>   *Then translate! . . .*
>   *More important than any*
>   *poetry—any crap . . .*
>   *words . . . words are*
>   *ridiculous for those*
>   *who've heard the music*
>   *of Orpheus.*

>   **ANNE-MARIE:**
>   *But you're drunk,*
>   *Monsieur Sartre!*

Boris appears on the small stage in the back of the club. Just as two drummers, in traditional West African garb begin playing drums.

>   **JP:**
>   *I'm not drunk. I'm*
>   *bewitched!*

Boris adjusts the microphone.

>   **BORIS:**
>   *Here is your*
>   *champagne!*

A young poet takes the stage. He begins reading from a book, over the drums.

POET:

*Hélé helélé the King
is a great king let his
majesty deign to look
up my anus to see if it
contains diamonds let
his majesty deign to
explore my mouth to
see how many carats it
contains laugh tom-tom
laugh tom-tom
I carry the king's litter
I roll out the king's
carpet I am the king's
carpet*

ANNE-MARIE:

(to Miles)
He thought you were
amazing too.

POET (V.O.) cont':

*sacred tom-toms
laughing about your rat
and hyena teeth under
the very nose of the
missionaries
tom-toms of salvation
who don't give a damn
about all the salvation
armies
tom-toms of the forest
tom-toms of the desert
black still virginal
muttered by each stone
unbeknownst to the*

disaster—my fever
weep tom-tom
weep tom-tom

JP (cont'):
All in all, I am in the
world and the world is
in me and this is what
the Prince of Darkness
breathes into our
mediocre world of hell
in which he lives. He
whispers: your language
is a dead language for
the dead, for mediocrity.
Anne-Marie, translate!

Miles's head is spinning between the drums and voices.

ANNE-MARIE:
(pointing to Juliette as
she arrives with drinks)
You! You're in love with
Eurydice!

POET cont':
Ni jour ni nuit
Ceci n'est pas un roman
Il n'y a jamais de roman
dans le coeur des
coffres-forts

JP:
Her! Oh no it's not
Eurydice! You think it's
death, but it's not death.

215

> *Death is the mirror. She*
> *is a witch, bewitched!*

Juliette hands Miles a drink and begins dancing wildly, as the mood of the room shifts.

The drummers begin playing more fiercely.

> **POET cont':**
> *roll roll deep roll soft*
> *tom-toms speechless*
> *deliriums*
> *russet lions without*
> *manes processions*
> *of thirst stench of the*
> *backwaters at night*
> *tom-toms that protect*
> *my three souls my brain*
> *my heart my liver*
> *harsh tom-toms that*
> *maintain on high my*
> *dwelling of water of*
> *wind of iodine of stars*
> *over the blasted rock of*
> *my black head*

Miles is transfixed.

> **POET:**
> *and you brother*
> *tom-tom for whom*
> *sometimes all day long*
> *I keep a word now hot*
> *now cool in my mouth*
> *like the little-known*
> *taste of vengeance tom-*

> *toms of kalahari*
> *tom-toms of Good Hope*
> *capping the cape with*
> *your threats*
> *O tom-tom of Zululand*
> *Tom-tom of Shaka*
> *tom tom tom*
> *tom tom tom*

Men and women moving wildly, their eyes rolling to the backs of their heads.

POET cont':
> *King our mountains are*
> *mares in heat caught*
> *in the full convulsion of*
> *bad blood*
> *King our plains are rivers*
> *vexed by the rotting*
> *provisions drifting in*
> *from the sea and from*
> *your caravels*
> *King our stones are*
> *lamps burning with a*
> *dragon widow hope*
> *King our trees are the*
> *unfurled shape taken by*
> *a flame too big for our*
> *hearts too weak for a*
> *dungeon*

Juliette and Miles are both staring at the stage.

MILES (V.O.):
Americans think the
beat era started in

America. But I suspect
that the origin of the
beat is like the origin of
anything else you wanna
put your finger on.

POET con't:

Laugh laugh then tom-
toms of Kaffirland
like the scorpion's
beautiful question mark
drawn in pollen on the
canvas of the sky and of
our brains at midnight
like the shiver of a sea
reptile charmed by
the anticipation of bad
weather
of the little upside-down
laugh of the sea in the
sunken ship's gorgeous
portholes

MILES (V.O.):

Paris was special
because they didn't try
to cloud the origin.
At least, that's how it
seemed at the time.

The drummers are working up a sweat.

Juliette's bedroom.

Juliette dances with her hips.
Miles's fingers gently playing the back of Juliette's legs like an upright
bass. He sits on the edge of a bed, arms wrapped around her, as she
stands pressed against him.

Juliette collapses over Miles.

A phonograph beside the bed plays a soft Ellington.

The open window shows the blue sky of a perfect Spring night.

The moon is waxing, not quite full.

Morning. Juliette's room.
Birds are singing outside the window.

Miles slowly opens his eyes and finds Juliette kissing his toes, feet, ankles, moving up his leg with each kiss.

Juliette straddles Miles.

He looks up at Juliette. Is he dreaming?

Juliette examines his face, like a painting with hidden messages.

> **JULIETTE:**
> (mouths)
> Giacometti.

Miles regards Juliette closely, the curve of her neck and shoulder, his hand on her thigh, waist, and sides . . .

Later.
Juliette begins searching her closet and the floor for a dress.

Miles sits on the bed, watching Juliette, and then begins browsing the records near the phonograph beside the bed.

Miles places a flamenco record on the phonograph.

Juliette begins to lift and hold each article of clothing with the dramatic flare of a toreador.

Miles looks on, enchanted and clueless.

Juliette pulls a black dress over her head and becomes a flamenco dancer.

Miles follows Juliette with his eyes as she claps and steps around the room.

Miles begins clapping with Juliette.

Miles, naked, jumps out of the bed and charges Juliette like a bull. They spin and land near the open window.

Miles looks down and sees a view that he recognizes . . . the sidewalk cafe, the street.

MILES:
Wait.

He looks around the room and again out the window.

He bends down and looks through the records again. Boom. Bessie Smith.

Miles grabs his stuff, walks to the door. He glances at Juliette who is putting on a dress, before walking out the door without saying a word.

Juliette freezes.

A moment passes before a soft trumpet is heard coming from outside. Juliette runs to the window, looks down at the sidewalk. No Miles. She looks to her left. Miles is leaning on the windowsill of the room beside hers, playing softly.

Juliette leans casually out the window and begins to hum.

A few moments pass before Juliette eases out of her room and into Miles's . . .

Late Morning. Sidewalk cafe.
Miles and Juliette downstairs at the cafe, seated at a table, exhausted and dazed from making love. They look at each other long and hard. They don't smile when they lock eyes. They are long past common courtesies and shocked by the speed of it.

Boris approaches the table, ruffled like he hasn't slept.

> **JULIETTE:**
> Bonjour, Boris!

> **BORIS:**
> Ah Toutoune.
> (Boris kisses Juliette's
> two cheeks)
> Miles.
> (Boris kisses Miles's two
> cheeks)

Miles, dazed, silently observes the customary greeting.

Boris sits, softly eyeing the two, as if calculating them, without saying a word. Juliette and Miles regard Boris and then each other.

> **BORIS:**
>
> . . .

                              JULIETTE:

                                . . .

                              MILES:

                                . . .

JP walks up to the table, greets the three of them and takes a seat.

                              JP:
                              (to Boris)
                              Holy Saint Francis, what
                              change is here!

Juliette and Miles take hands.

                              BORIS:
                              Not to worry. Love is the
                              only opiate that doesn't
                              kill.

                              JP:
                              A man after my own
                              heart.

A boy holding a red balloon running by, lights up when he sees Miles and
waves.

                              CHILD:
                              Hello!

Composition.
A soft trumpet comes in as Miles's eyes follow the passing child.

The conversation continues, but fades into a choral ambiance.

                                    MILES (V.O.):
                                    And just like that, it
                                    dawned on me that *the
                                    world* was bigger than
                                    my world.

Another horn comes in, complementing the first.

Juliette grabs Miles's hand and pulls him away from the table and into the
street

A group of children run by. The music comes to life.

A soft orchestra underscores, following the melody of the trumpet. A
morning stroll, cool.

                                    MILES (V.O.):
                                    I'm not sure if it was
                                    because I was in Paris,
                                    or simply because I was
                                    out of America, but I
                                    began to see people and
                                    the world differently.

Juliette and Miles pass an array of Saint-Germain types, poor, bohemian,
vendors, soldiers . . .

                                    MILES (V.O.):
                                    I began to pay attention.

Juliette and Miles pass a church where an old lady is feeding and talking
to birds. The birds fly up and close to Juliette's head.

A swoop of blackbirds flailing in slow motion around the head of Juliette.
Her big eyes staring up at the birds as they fly close and around her
head.

                                        MILES (V.O.):
                                        I began to notice the
                                        signs.

Miles and Juliette running down the street and into their hotel. They try
to contain their pace in the lobby before running up the stairs and into
Juliette's room. The moment they enter, they are all over each other,
pulling off their clothes, and making love. They are passionate, enthralled
by the vision of the other, curious, bestial.

Backstage Salle Pleyel.
Juliette looking through the stage door at Miles playing onstage.

Miles is in form.

The song finishes. The audience applauds.

Miles sees Juliette as he walks offstage. Touched by a ray of the spotlight,
his shadow grows on her.

Juliette faces Miles, on the verge of tears. An unexpected love.

Miles reaches out with his free hand and touches Juliette's face.

They kiss beside the doorway as the musicians finish and begin walking
backstage.

Backstage. Miles's dressing room.
Miles closes the door behind him as he enters.

He puts his trumpet down as he kisses her.

                                        MILES:
                                        I couldn't think of
                                        anything but you, up
                                        there.

Reste avec moi.

Miles traces Juliette's face with his finger, blows into her eyes. They kiss.

Their attraction is animal.

Juliette's face pressed against the wall, Miles moves slow, close behind her.

Miles and Juliette walking home. Night.
Juliette leads Miles to an unknown destination.
They walk into a small room in a basement with half-finished sculptures in various states, an artist's studio. The artist greets Juliette as if an old friend. Miles observes the sculptures. Juliette observes Miles.

They say good-bye to the artist and are back on the street.

Juliette takes Miles into a small club where the people are seated in a circle, watching a couple dance, tango. The man is dragging the woman across the floor by her hair.

Seine. Dawn.
Juliette and Miles walking along the left bank of the Seine at dawn.

Juliette sits on the pavement beside the river. Miles joins her.

Juliette and Miles look out over the water, alone on the planet, before the city has come to life.

Miles lays his head in Juliette's lap.

Juliette traces his face, slowly, with her finger.

JULIETTE (V.O.):
It's been six days since I

*came to this exact spot
and, without knowing,
asked for you . . . Miles.)*

The light plays on the water.

A family of swans float by.

The moon, almost full, is fully visible as the sun rises.

Pont Saint-Louis. Morning.
Miles and Juliette holding hands, crossing the Pont Saint-Louis to Isle Saint-Louis.

Workers and students pass in groups.

A small group of teens, on their way to school, exchange whispers as Miles and Juliette approach.

A young girl leaves the group and approaches them.

> **GIRL:**
> Excuse me. Are you
> Charlie Parker?

> **MILES:**
> Um.

Juliette laughs.

> **GIRL:**
> We love your music.
> (to Juliette)
> Vous êtes vraiment beau
> ensemble.

Merci.

Miles and Juliette continue walking.

A young homeless man sleeps on a bench.

Two white American soldiers pass.

One of the soldiers whispers and laughs to the other while glancing at Miles and Juliette.

Miles stiffens.

Juliette turns and sees the soldiers.

One of the soldiers smiles at Juliette.

Juliette turns and kisses Miles.

Inside a cafe. Morning.
Miles and Juliette are seated near the window of a small cafe.

Two empty coffee cups are on their table.

The waiter approaches with two fresh cups.

Miles bends close to the coffee to smell it.

Juliette taps Miles on the back of his head.

Miles's nose dips into the coffee.

Juliette laughs and then mimes smelling her coffee cup like a bouquet of roses.

Miles dips his finger in his coffee and rubs it on her nose before kissing it off.

Miles takes Juliette's hand.

Juliette looks down at their fingers together.

Miles notices a woman, who has stopped, outside, just in front of them, staring in the window.

Miles looks behind himself unsure as to if the woman is staring at him.

Juliette notices the woman, whose eyes are going deeper and deeper into concentration as she stares through the window at something or someone just behind them.

Juliette turns around, making eye contact with a man, sitting at a table not far behind them.

The man glances up at the woman in the window and is suddenly agitated, awkward.

He calls the waiter over.

The woman outside starts calling out behind her, while pointing to the man.

> **WOMAN:**
> Eh! Eh! Je lui reconnais.
> Je lui reconnais!

He spills his glass of water, reaching for his coat and hat.

He places money on the table and rushes out the door, brushing past the woman as she calls out:

> **WOMAN:**
> Collabo! C'est un
> collabo! I recognize him.

Two men run towards the man.

The man breaks into a sprint.

> **VOICES:**
> Collabo! Collabo!

There is a small commotion outside.

More people give chase.

The woman is still by the window, talking to people that have gathered around her.

Miles looks at Juliette, confused. "What's happening?"

Juliette is white.

Saint-Michel. Early afternoon.
The height of the May sun in the blue sky.

Juliette walks with her head on Miles's shoulder.

Their walk is a little slowed down by the love fatigue.

Miles observes ruins, the architecture of churches and buildings, small bookshops and cafes, and in all of these places he notices soldiers.

Soldiers in cafes.

Soldiers in the streets.

Soldiers in formation.

Soldiers on patrol.

Juliette, still disturbed from earlier, is distant to the outside world but attentive to Miles.

She squeezes Miles's hand and looks him in the eye.

An old woman smiles as they pass.

Miles looks concerned.

A small record store. Mid-day.
Miles and Juliette enter a very small store crowded with records and posters.

The opera *Norma* of Bellini is playing from the speakers.

The man working behind the counter squints curiously at them.

> **JULIETTE:**
> Bonjour.

> **MAN:**
> Bonjour.

Miles sees the jazz bin and goes directly to it. He browses titles quickly but keeps looking up. He turns to Juliette.

> **MILES:**
> (pointing to the
> speakers)
> Who's this?

> **JULIETTE:**
> Maria Callas, La Callas.

She walks towards the register and points to the album. Miles buys the record.

> **MILES:**
> All right. Let's get out
> of here.

Two soldiers enter as they exit.

Juliette and Miles walk back into the street.

Saint-Michel. Early afternoon.
We are behind Miles and Juliette as they walk up a large avenue.

The sun is bright.

Miles, tired, puts his head on Juliette's head.

They stop to look in the windows of shops here and there.

> **JULIETTE:**
> (joining her palms
> together and laying her
> head on top)
> Tu . . . veux . . . dormir?

> **MILES:**
> (shaking his head)
> Oui Mademoiselle
> Juliette.

                                            JULIETTE:
                                            (grabbing his hand)
                                            Viens, par là!

They take a little street on the right.

They walk up the little street as if it's impossible to climb.

Juliette stops in front of a building.

Miles looks up and smiles.

Cinema. Mid-Afternoon.

                                            JULIETTE:
                                            *Hello, I'd like two tickets
                                            please, for, hmmm, Le
                                            Chien enragé.*
                                            (She looks at the posters
                                            on the wall *and chooses)*
                                            . . . *Le chien enragé.*

                                            CINÉPHILE:
                                            *Very good choice,
                                            mademoiselle, but the
                                            film has already begun.*

                                            JULIETTE:
                                            (winking at him)
                                            *Yes, but still, we want to
                                            see it,* tout de suite.

She winks and smiles at him.

                                            MILES:
                                            Toot sweet, Môsieur!

*As you wish, here are
your tickets.
The little theater at the
bottom of the steps.
Enjoy the film.*
(he winks at her)

Miles winks at the guy and follows Juliette into a little dark hallway.

Miles opens the door and they enter a dark room floodlit by the image's projection.

Few people are seated here and there, couples and individuals, all lit by the movie.

They find two empty seats and sit, silently.

It is almost the middle of the movie.

Miles is amazed by the first image he sees, the modernity of the style, the costumes, the music, the way they talk . . .

MILES (V.O.):
Style and influence.
Love and inspiration.

Juliette is looking at Miles.

MILES (V.O.):
Don't look at me like
you don't know what I'm
talking about.

Juliette lays her head on Miles's shoulder.

> **MILES (V.O.):**
> It is an assessment
> of sensibilities, an
> acquiring of taste.

Miles takes notice of the people in the theater: old couples, young students, lonely men and women, all looking precious in the light.

> **MILES (V.O.):**
> Every seat, every life in
> the theater is a story, a
> song.

Miles plunges back in his seat, trying to close his eyes but he's too captivated by the scene.

Juliette closes her eyes.

Miles closes his eyes.

> **MILES (V.O.) cont':**
> I had listened without
> hearing. I heard it, but I
> couldn't tell what I was
> listening to. I kept trying
> to place the melody,
> trying to find one until
> it appeared bluish and
> swirling clear as split
> of sea and sky and I
> realized it all had been a
> long introduction.

We continue to hear the movie as we witness:

A few seats away, a young woman with tears in her eyes, turns her head toward them, as they sleep, and then goes back to the movie.

On the screen, the movie credits roll.

A few people begin to leave the theater.

Miles wakes up in a flash.

He looks around and gently settles a kiss on Juliette's mouth, as she sleeps.

She opens her eyes.

Taxi. Paris. Evening.
Miles and Juliette are in the back of a taxi heading to the concert.

They can't keep their hands off of each other.

The taxi driver, an old Frenchman, is disturbed by their public display of affection.

> **TAXI DRIVER:**
> (looking in the rearview mirror)
> *Hmm. Hmmm. A bit of prudence, please. This isn't Africa.*

> **JULIETTE:**
> *We'll get out here.*

The taxi stops.

> **TAXI DRIVER:**
> *No problem. That will be five francs.*

JULIETTE:
On vous fera livrer des
bananes, du con.
(To Miles)
Sortons.

Miles and Juliette exit the taxi.

TAXI DRIVER:
J'appelle la police!

Juliette approaches the driver's window with a smile and punches him in
the face.

JULIETTE:
Ça c'est le pourboire.
Maintenant, appellez la
police!

Miles stands stupefied, on the curb, holding his trumpet case.

Juliette grabs Miles's hand and starts running.

Champs-Élysées. Night.
Miles and Juliette running down Champs-Élysées.

Miles and Juliette approaching Salle Pleyel on foot and out of breath.

They're laughing.

There's a long line outside the concert hall.

Juliette, still in form from her successful bout and getaway, jumps right
into character as Miles's bodyguard as they walk towards the entrance.

Miles sees Bird looking lost in the crowd.

MILES:
Hey man, what you doin
out here, Bird?

BIRD:
I don't feel good, man.

JULIETTE:
Ça va?

BIRD:
(Smiling. Trying.)
Ça va.

Miles gives a knowing look.

MILES:
Come on, man.

Miles drags Bird inside with him and Juliette.

Backstage. Pre-show.
Miles is sitting Bird down on a couch in an empty dressing room.

MILES:
Drink something, man.

Juliette appears in the doorway with Boris.

BORIS:
(concerned)
Miles, Charlie isn't
feeling well?

Miles whispers something into Boris's ear.

MILES:
(to Bird)
Just stay here, man.

They exit.

Miles's Dressing Room. Backstage. After the show.
Juliette claps quietly for Miles as he enters after the show.

Miles closes the door behind him, puts his trumpet down and kisses her.

There's a knock on the door.

MILES:
(with an attitude, playful)
Who is it?

CLARKE:
It's Clarke.

Juliette and Miles straighten up before turning to the door.

MILES:
Aw, come in, man.

CLARKE:
(playfully)
I hope I'm not disturbing
anything.

MILES:
(looking for a bottle)
You want something to
drink, man?

CLARKE:
(holding his glass up)
I'm already drinking.

Clarke sits down.

Miles sits.

Juliette walks out of the room.

Miles watches her leave.

CLARKE:
That was something,
man.

MILES:
Yeah.

CLARKE:
(after a slow pause)
Miles, I'm staying.

MILES:
You staying?

CLARKE:
I'm staying. Yeah, I'm
staying. You see it. You
see it, just like me,
man. I was on that
stage playing tonight
and thinking, "What
the hell I got to go
back for, except for a
few sessions here and

there?" I don't think I
have it in me to know
that some less tiresome
shit exists over here and
I'm over there fighting.
For what? They ain't
the same as the white
folks over here. This is a
different world.

MILES:
Yeah.

CLARKE:
It's a different world,
man. And shit ain't
changing over there.
Shit ain't changing,
shit ain't changing, shit
ain't changing over
there.

MILES:
I see changes, like
the music. Man, shit
changing everywhere.

CLARKE:
No, it isn't. Don't be
fooled, Miles. Shit ain't
changing over there. But
you see it. They can see
us. And we people over
here. Look at your girl.
She just love you, like
it's normal. And you ain't

cute, Miles. You ain't
cute, Miles, anywhere.

We hear laughter from the next room.

MILES:
Fuck you, man.
(Miles laughs)
But you right. It's
beautiful over here.

Juliette enters with two bottles of wine.

Clarke gets up to exit.

CLARKE:
All right man, I wanted
you to be the first to
know.

Juliette pours wine into two glasses and hands one to Miles before she
sits.

Miles regards Juliette like an apparition.

CLARKE:
Don't you want to
try one of them new
numbers tomorrow
night?

MILES:
The rest of the guys
don't know they parts.

                              CLARKE:
                              We probably got time to
                              rehearse tomorrow.

Miles looks at Juliette.

Clarke bursts out in laughter.

The rising sound of saxophone comes from a nearby room. It rises and
falls through the scales in multiple variations.

Miles takes a sip of his wine.

                              MILES (V.O.):
                              The hounds were rising
                              up in me.

The sound becomes increasingly winding and intense.

Miles and Clarke share a look.

                              JULIETTE:
                              Quoi?

                              MILES:
                                  . . .

Miles slowly rises and leads Juliette and Clarke into the hallway, just as
Moody, Boris, Michelle, and others are beginning to gather in the hallway,
all wondering, "What's going on?"

Miles and Juliette lead the group in the direction of the sound.

They walk softly, like nosey neighbors, trying to get a closer listen to a
domestic dispute next door.

The sound of the sax rises and swirls in unimagined velocity and range, like a wolf howling Rachmaninov.

They walk to the far end of the hallway until they reach an open door.

Bird is pacing in a dark room, full of sweat, shirtsleeves rolled up, blowing through his sax.

His pace is wobbly. He is in and out of tune.

Everyone is quiet, as if not wanting to disturb a sleepwalker. They share varying expressions of awe and concern.

Miles looks back and silently assures the crowd.

Boris is caught with a dance twitch.

Moody is holding his sax.

Clarke in a trance, imagining his drum beneath.

Bird plays non-stop.

Miles gestures to Juliette ("wait, I'll be right back") and hurries back to his dressing room to grab his trumpet.

Boris pops out of his twerk.

> **BORIS:**
> What's going on?

> **MILES:**
> It's the spirit.

Miles grabs his trumpet from his dressing room and walks through the crowd back to Bird's room.

Juliette is at a poetry reading, captivated.

Miles begins to play soft clear notes in harmony with Bird's wail as it pushes through memories of Negro spirituals to modern forms of prayer, until it is clearly, and distinctly, a man crying, screaming to be understood.

Miles's soft playing brings Bird's playing to lesser and lesser decibels.

Bird begins to play softly with Miles.

Miles fades his sound to an end.

Bird stops.

There is a brief moment of silence before Bird opens his eyes and looks at Miles.

> **BIRD:**
> Hey man, who stopped
> the music?

Foil and a burnt spoon are on the table.

Berny's car. Night. Paris. Full Moon.
Miles, Juliette, Tadd, Moody, and Clarke are in a convertible car with Berny, a white American living in Paris, the bass player of the group.

Moody sits in the front with Berny.

> **CLARKE:**
> Man, this city is
> something else.

MOODY:
Yeah, it sure is. I been here a year and all I can say is . . . no racist police checking my arms or my privates, no losing my cabaret card. We people over here.

CLARKE:
Yep.

MOODY:
And the women ain't bad either.

MILES:
What about you Berny? Anybody called you nigger over here yet?

Laughter.

BERNY:
Not yet, Miles, but a few have been starting to call me "Mingus."

More laughter.

MILES:
Well, you should kiss the next person that calls you that.

BERNY:
(without missing a
beat)
Juliette, est-ce que tu as
déjà entendu parler de
quelqu'un qui s'appelle
Mingus?

JULIETTE:
Mein goose?

Laughter.

MILES:
Nice try, mothafucka.

BERNY:
(to Juliette)
C'est un musicien.

CLARKE:
Musicien? That's
"musician"?

Berny and Moody answer at the same time.

BERNY:
Yep.

MOODY:
It's a mortician.

JULIETTE:
(to Miles)
Magicien.

The lights of city as they cross the bridge into the Left Bank.

                                        JULIETTE:
                                        Arrêtez

The car jerks to a halt. Juliette pops out, grabbing Miles's hand.

                                        JULIETTE:
                                        Viens.

Miles follows Juliette. Juliette takes off her shoes to walk barefoot.

Miles and Juliette walk hand in hand along the Seine.

A family of swans float by. Black waves ripple around them. The moon is practically full overhead.

A flock of birds fly overhead and nearby at the feet of an old woman sitting at a small table. She gestures to the young couple.

Juliette holds Miles close.

                                        JULIETTE:
                                        Why do we need an old
                                        woman to explain what
                                        we already know?

Miles traces her lips as she speaks. He loves the sounds of the words coming out of her mouth.

                                        JULIETTE:
                                        You will pay for making
                                        me love you.

Miles and Juliette walking through a small alleyway at night. Juliette is humming a soft melody. Miles walks and listens, enraptured.

Juliette's hotel room.
Juliette and Miles in bed. The moon outside their window.

Juliette has her head on Miles's chest, asleep. Miles slowly closes his eyes.

Pine Bluff, Arkansas.
We are on the back of a horse trotting down a dirt trail, through tall green trees in rural Arkansas.

Other horses run wild in front of us.

We see their heels kick up dust and patches of grass.

The branches of large pines hang like spiderwebs over the trail.

We approach an abandoned wooden shack and stop.

The other horses run ahead.

We jump off the horse.

An old, leathered man in native dress walks by, leading a horse from a leather strap. The man looks straight ahead and does not turn from the path.

We watch them walk away.

We approach the door of the shack.

We open the door.

Inside the Shack.

Men and women in brown horse masks are seated casually in rows of chairs in an open wooden space. Children sit on their parents' laps and play on the floor.

We are seated at a desk by the entrance, beside the receptionist.

The receptionist, a well-dressed brown woman, does not look in our direction. Her stocking legs fit neatly under the desk. Her skirt is hiked enough to see her knees.

In front of us, pieces of coloring paper and crayons are spread out over half of the desk. The crayons seem small. The papers are covered with crayon sketches of horses.

A man in a white horse mask and white suit seems huge as he approaches the table.

> **BUSINESSMAN:**
> I need to see Dr. Davis.
> Immediately.

> **RECEPTIONIST (V.O.):**
> I'm sorry, but the "Do Not Disturb" sign is on the door, which means I am not to interrupt Dr. Davis at the moment. (grabbing a small pad and pencil) Would you like to leave a note for him?

The man looks around the room, huffs, and walks quickly towards a door at the far end.

A small sign on the door reads: *Dr. Corrine, Reader, Healer.*

We open the door and enter a small dim room with a desk, lit by candles.

Tarot cards are spread across the table.

A dark muscular woman sits behind a small wooden desk.

We sit in a chair in front of the old woman.

We look down at our hands.

We are holding a trumpet.

We lift the trumpet to our mouth.

Juliette's hotel room.
Miles and Juliette asleep in bed.

Juliette is on her back. Miles is curled beside her, mouth pressed against Juliette's shoulder, clutching her arm.

Close on Miles pressing his fingertips into Juliette's arm like the keys of a trumpet.

A hand comes from Miles's side of the bed and taps him on his shoulder.

Miles turns. He is full of sweat. He has difficulty keeping his eyes open.

> **MILES:**
> I'm okay. I'm okay.

Miles turns back towards Juliette.

She's not there.

The room is dark.

Juliette approaches the bed with a glass of water.

> **JULIETTE:**
> Tiens.

She hands Miles the glass.

Miles drinks.

Juliette's silhouette.

Miles hands back the half-empty glass.

Juliette throws the water in Miles's face.

Miles snatches Juliette like a wild beast.

> **MALE VOICE:**
> No, Miles, NO!

Wooden Shack—Arkansas.
Dr. Davis, Miles's father, is trying to unwrap Miles's arms from around his waist.

He is standing beside the bed where Miles, covered in sweat, is tossing and turning.

He uses a towel to wipe Miles's face and exits.

The door slams behind him.

Miles bolt up in bed, eyes wide open.

He is in a single bed in the far end of an empty wooden shack.

There is an empty glass and pitcher of water beside the bed.

Miles sits up on the bed, places his bare feet on the floor.

He sees sunlight seeping through the cracks of the wood-planked walls.

Miles lies back down and closes his eyes.

Juliette's finger traces Miles's face.

> **JULIETTE (V.O.):**
> *I know you are going
> to do as you want.
> But I want you to stay
> with me. We have lived
> through a war and
> maybe it is that your war
> continues at home.
> But this can be your
> home. I am yours, if you
> want me.*

Miles opens his eyes. The beams of light, through the cracks in the wall are like lasers, over and around him. He sits up, pours himself a glass of water and hears the birds singing outside.

> **JULIETTE (V.O.):**
> Was it your dream or
> mine?
> The trumpet calls to
> war. The bird flies to
> safety.

Miles stands, examines his face in the mirror, before picking up his trumpet. He opens the shutters. Sunlight bursts through. He looks out at the trees, the birds, horses in the distance, and lifts the trumpet to his mouth.

Personal

Counterfeit Colonel
of one-man army seeks
heiress of Wonderbread
for deli of dogmas.

Farm-raised catfish of
fathomless beginnings
seeks mermaid of
primordial waters
for upstream marathon
in depthless stream
of consciousness.

Armless conductor
of Styrofoam orchestra
seeks brass-sectioned robot
for radio broadcast
of new symphony
written in blood.
C# for details.

Dead organist
seeks prenatal
plastic surgeon
for "everybody
knows" job in
purgatorial pursuit
of skeletal bones
sent down the
wrong pipe.

Handyman foot doctor
with specialty in dog paws
seeks Elizabeth Taylor–type
for long walks in circles
and pumice stone skipping
in the Fountain of Youth.

Young NGH seeks truth.

Acknowledgments

US (a.) is a commissioned work that would not have come about without the enthusiasm of Ed Schlesinger, Jacob Hoye, and the tireless efforts of Charlotte Gusay. I would like to thank them and their respective teams for working on my behalf (including Jennifer Bergstrom, John Paul Jones, Davina Mock-Maniscalco, Shelly Powell, and Christine Buckley), along with Dave Guenette and Sol Guy. I also owe a great deal to my creative inspirations: to the legacy of artists like Imamu Amiri Baraka, Tupac Shakur, Nina Simone, Octavia Butler, James Baldwin, Boris Vian, Charlie Parker, Miles Davis, and Juliette Greco (who I depict as fictional characters in this work), and others whose lives and works have charged my imagination and fueled my perseverance. I'd also like to thank thinkers, teachers, and activists, like my mother, Juanita Sealy-Williams, who have instilled in me a proper sense of rebellion, resilience, and an insistence on seeing social injustice eradicated.

Finally, I thank Anisia Uzeyman-Williams, my wife and creative partner, whose insight and aesthetic mastery informs and heightens the reach of this outstretched middle finger.

Permissions

Excerpt by Imamu Amiri Baraka (Leroi Jones) *Raise, Race, Rays, Raze: Essays Since 1965.* Used by Permission of Random House and the Baraka Estate. Copyright © 1969, 1970, 1971 by Leroi Jones.

Excerpt from "Changes"
Words and Music by Tupac Shakur, Deon Evans and Bruce Hornsby. Copyright © 1998 UNIVERSAL MUSIC CORP., UNIVERSAL MUSIC - Z SONGS, BACK ON POINT MUSIC and ZAPPO MUSIC. All Rights for BACK ON POINT MUSIC Controlled and Administered by UNIVERSAL MUSIC - Z SONGS. All Rights for ZAPPO MUSIC Administered by SONY/ATV MUSIC PUBLISHING LLC, 424 Church Street, Suite 1200, Nashville, TN, 37219. All Rights Reserved Used by Permission—contains elements of "The Way It Is." Reprinted by Permission of Hal Leonard Corporation.

Photo of Juanita Sealy-Williams by Dick DeMarsico (circa 1968). Courtesy of the U.S. Library of Congress/*New York World-Telegram & Sun* Newspaper Photograph Collection (Reproduction Number: LC-USZ62-134715). This collection is part of the public domain photo collection donated to the Library of Congress by the *New York World-Telegram & Sun.*